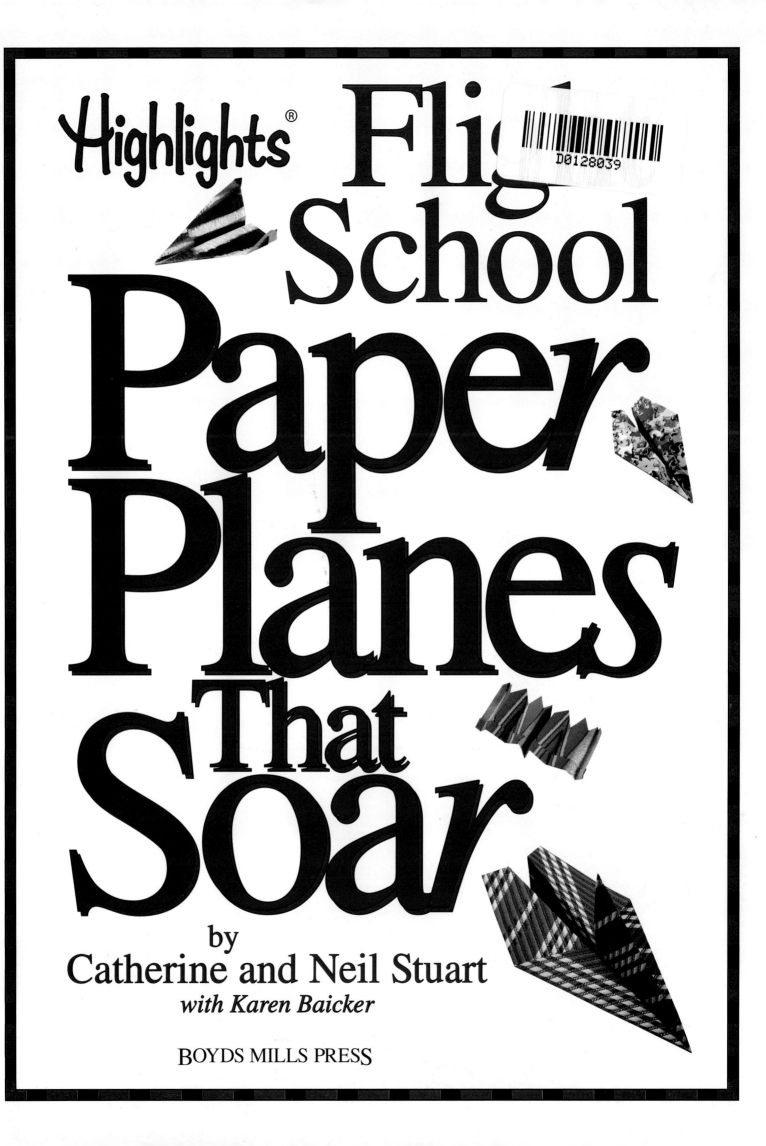

Highlights® Flight School Paper Planes That Soar

by
Catherine and Neil Stuart
with Karen Baicker

BOYDS MILLS PRESS

The publisher is grateful to the following individuals for sharing their knowledge
of the science of flight for the preparation of this book:

Scott Eberhardt, PhD
Associate Professor of Aeronautics and Astronautics
University of Washington–Seattle

and

Milton W. Cole, PhD
Distinguished Professor of Materials Science and Engineering
Distinguished Professor of Physics
The Pennsylvania State University

Published by Boyds Mills Press, Inc.
A Highlights Company
815 Church Street
Honesdale, Pennsylvania 18431
Printed in China

Publisher Cataloging-in-Publication Data (U.S.)

Stuart, Catherine.
Paper planes that soar : Highlights Flight School / Catherine and Neil Stuart.
[256] p. : col. photos. ;   cm.
Summary: Provides information on the science of flight and how to build paper airplanes. Includes paper for making airplanes
as well as a pullout poster with flight games.
ISBN 1-59078-388-3
1. Paper airplanes—Juvenile literature. I. Neil Stuart. II. Title.
745.592 dc22   TL778.S783 2005

First edition, 2005
The text of this book is set in 16-point Times Roman.

Visit our Web site at www.boydsmillspress.com

10 9 8 7 6 5 4 3 2 1

Table of Contents

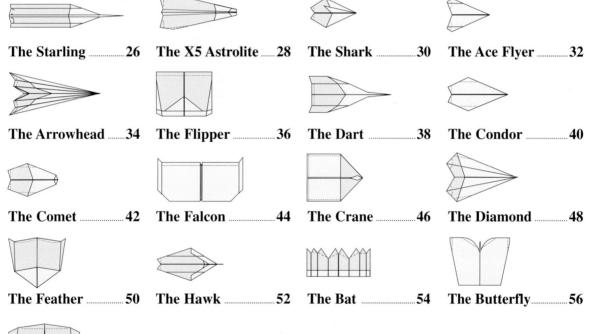

Introduction

Wings of Promise

Every paper airplane starts as a blank slate, a fresh piece of paper, full of possibilities. Each fold is creased with hope, with a soaring vision of flight.

And then, all too often, that dream of graceful gliding is dashed by reality. You launch the plane. It veers left and quickly nose-dives into a chair. You crumple it into a ball and throw it in the wastebasket. And if you're an optimist, you grab a fresh piece of paper and begin again.

This book is written for you optimists, with a promise. Your planes can soar—even the one that took a dive! If you understand some basic, simple principles behind the science of flight, you can turn a crasher into a glider. Adjust a wing, crimp a tail, add some weight to the nose, and your plane can regain its former promise.

"Plane" and Simple

Part of the beauty of making paper airplanes is how simple the whole process can be. You don't need any fancy equipment— just a single sheet of paper. The paper itself contains all the properties necessary for flight.

A successful paper airplane depends on

- sound aerodynamics,
- careful and precise folding,
- a good throw, and
- informed adjustments.

This book has been designed to meet all of those criteria. Beyond that, it is based on one guiding goal: for you to have fun.

Flying a paper airplane should be liberating, not frustrating.

Why Fly?

Paper airplanes are fun, but they offer many additional benefits, as you can see from the following top ten list.

Top Ten Reasons to Fly Paper Airplanes

- It doesn't cost any money.
- You'll learn about aerodynamics.
- You can recycle used papers.
- You don't need batteries.
- You'll practice following directions.
- You can practice your aim.
- You can develop your folding skills.
- You'll learn to think like a NASA scientist.
- You'll learn about spatial relations.
- It's safer than throwing a football in the house.

And guess what? They're all true!

Using This Book

So grab some paper, and let's make some planes!

Before you do, you might want to check these tips for using this book. You'll find some special papers in the back that can be used with any of the models shown or for your own creations. They'll make your plane look cool, but they won't make it fly any better. You can use any regular printer paper with just as much success. It's all in the folds and the throw.

In the pages that follow, you will enter Highlights Flight School. You'll learn about the history of paper planes, why they fly, the art of folding, and more. You'll earn your wings!

If you can't wait to get started, though, you can also jump right ahead to the models, starting on page 26. You can always return to the beginning pages along the way. You'll also find a pullout poster with paper-airplane games (see inside the back cover), which will allow you to share your love of flying (or your competitive spirit) with your friends.

Happy Flying!

About the Airplane Papers

Get to know the feel of your flight-ready airplane paper.

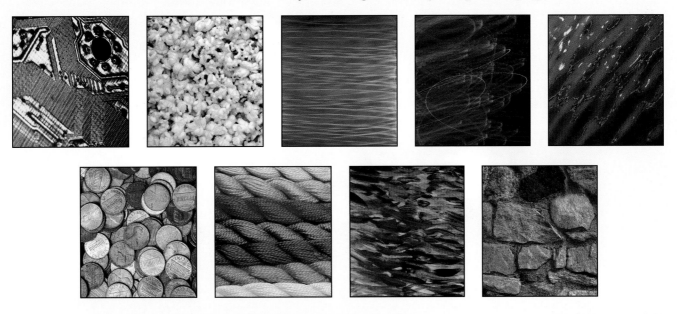

It's ideal for the planes in this book. Thinner paper may be too floppy; thicker paper may weigh the plane down (see page 12). You can check out wrapping paper, magazine pages, and other scrap paper to see if they're flightworthy.

Your flight-ready plane paper is perforated for easy removal.

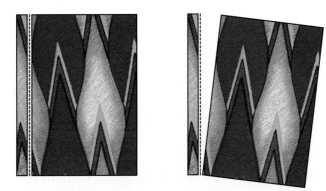

Create a soft crease along the perforation, then place your hand flat and firmly on the page, near the creased, perforated holes. Pull firmly and slowly away from the spine of the book.

The flight-ready plane paper included in this book measures 8½" x 12". The diagrams are based on that size but will work just fine with regular printer paper. You can find your flight-ready airplane paper after page 68.

Flight School

The History of Paper Airplanes

Long before the Wright brothers sputtered into flight, someone took a piece of paper and lofted it into the air. Perhaps it crashed into a column or a pyramid. And so, that person made a fold here or there and tried again.

Wilbur and Orville Wright first tested their plane by building a model kite. Today, flight engineers continue to test planes and rockets by using paper models.

No one knows for sure when paper airplanes were invented, but we do know that the Chinese invented paper. They also have been flying kites for over two thousand years. Their earliest kites, perhaps the first form of paper planes, were made from paper.

Paper airplanes became a hot item in the United States during the 1940s. Many materials were scarce, and toys were considered a trivial use of precious resources. So toy manufacturers began to create toys out of paper and wood again, as they had in previous decades. Toy airplanes became more sophisticated and were modeled after different aircraft.

Soon cutout airplane models were featured in the comic section of newspapers and as cereal-box giveaways. Eventually, toy companies went back to making toys out of metal, plastic, and other materials. But a craze had been born that continues even today.

Just as airplanes have come a long way since the Wright brothers, paper airplanes have developed into a science as well. In fact, paper airplanes have flown farther than the first flight of a real plane.

Times have changed, toys have changed, but some things will never change! Sending a piece of paper into flight is still magical. Even today, with all of the high-tech video games and electronic gizmos available, the simple paper airplane holds a fascination for kids and grown-ups alike. Right now, as you read this, someone, somewhere, is making a new fold here, a crimp there—and testing out a brand-new plane.

The Science of Flight

You don't get the keys to a Cessna and fly solo your first time out. Similarly, you can't be a successful paper-airplane pilot without some basic flight training. Over the next pages, you will acquire all the background and training needed to become an ace pilot.

Anyone who has ever watched a bird glide above the trees or a real plane take off has marveled at the gravity-defying wonder of flight. How do the bird and plane stay in the air?

The same essential mystery arises from watching a paper airplane soar through the air. And the same scientific principles of real planes guide a paper airplane's flight.

Although it is simple to take a sheet of paper, crease it a few times, and make a paper airplane, creating a great flyer is another story. To complete basic training, you need to master the following:

1. The principles of flight. The best paper airplanes are designed with knowledge of aerodynamics and what makes planes effective gliders.

2. Folding. Planes will fly well only if they are folded with care, attention to detail, and accuracy.

3. Launching. Even the best-made planes can flub without the proper launch. Knowing how to grip and toss each plane is essential for a good flight.

And, of course, **Steps 4**, **5**, and **6**: **Practice, Practice, Practice.** Our Flight School motto is Practice Makes Perfect. Remember, you have to record many hours of flight (see page 65) before you become an ace pilot.

Forces of Aerodynamics

A paper airplane is a special type of airplane called a *glider*. The forces of aerodynamics work a bit differently on gliders than they do on powered aircraft such as jet airplanes.

 Aerodynamics: The science of how air moves and how it creates forces on objects as they move through it.

For all airplanes, two forces work against flight. *Gravity* pulls down on planes, and *drag* tends to slow them down. Two other forces allow airplanes to take flight. *Lift* is an upward push, created by the wings. It works against gravity. *Thrust* is a continuous forward push, created by the jet engine or propeller. It counteracts drag.

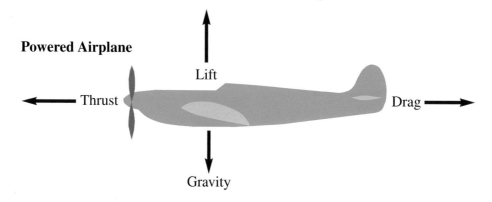

Powered Airplane

Lift

Thrust

Drag

Gravity

Thrust is the main difference between a jet airplane and a glider. Paper airplanes and other gliders do not use thrust. They follow a downward flight path. In fact, they cheat gravity, using its pull to gain speed, which adds lift.

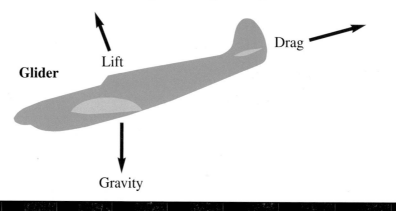

Drag

Lift

Glider

Gravity

How Wings Create Lift

Wings create lift by pushing downward on the air.
Notice that the front edge of each wing on an airplane is set higher than
the rear edge. This *angle of attack* pushes down on the air that passes under the
wing. That downward push on the air creates an upward push on the wing.

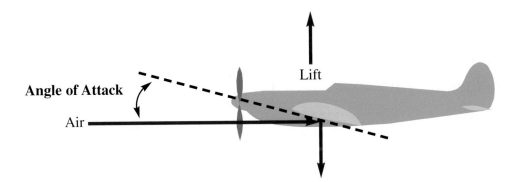

How Can You Reduce Drag?

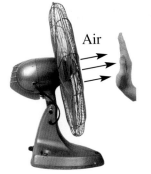

Have you ever placed your hand or a sheet of
cardboard in front of a fan? You can feel the same
forces that affect a wing moving through the air. If
you turn your hand so that your palm is flat against
the breeze, you will feel a lot of pressure pushing
back against your hand. That drag is caused by high
pressure against the palm of your hand plus a much
lower pressure area pulling on the back of it. If you
keep your hand parallel to the floor, you feel less
resistance because the air can flow smoothly around
it without a large area to push against or a large area
behind to form a low-pressure pull.

Can you turn your hand to an angle of attack   so that the moving air
will give your hand some lift? In order to get   lift, you have to
accept some drag. But you can find an angle of attack that gives the
most lift with the least amount of drag.

Traffic Control: Where to Fly

Planes don't fly in a vacuum. Flight is affected by the environment.
Pilots are glad to fly on a calm day and use extra caution during rainstorms.
And airports shut down altogether during ice storms.
For your paper airplanes, you'll need to take your environment into account.

Flying Outside

If you're outdoors, you'll need to consider the weather conditions.

1. Is it windy?

Wind can work to your advantage if you launch your plane in the
direction of the air flow. To tell which way the wind is blowing, wet your
finger and stick it in the air. You'll feel the direction of the breeze.
If you fly in the direction of the wind, you'll get a burst of extra speed.
Without much effort, your plane will fly a great distance.

If you throw the plane into the wind, there will be more resistance.
But the wind will provide extra lift, and your plane will fly higher. It may stay
aloft a long time, but it will not fly far.

2. Is it sunny?

A hot, sunny day creates currents of warm air rising from the ground.
Those currents can replace gravity as a source of power for flight. Have you ever
seen heat rising from a blacktop street or parking lot? Those surfaces heat up
faster than grass and can create more heat currents. Try flying a plane in
an unused parking lot or a blacktop area at a school.

3. Is it humid or raining?

Of course, a downpour will drench your plane. Even humid air
can make your plane soggy and add extra weight to it.
That will tend to pull your plane down.

Flying Inside

If you're indoors, you don't need to think about the climate and air current as much. But you still need to think about the surroundings.

1. Remember, safety first!

Flying paper airplanes is a lot safer than bungee jumping or flame throwing. Even so, those pointy tips can be sharp. Make sure to fly your plane away from people. You don't want a plane to hit someone.

2. Is there enough open space?

Paper-airplane contests often take place in gymnasiums or other large, empty spaces. If you can get permission to test your planes in your school gym, that would be ideal. If you're flying at home, try to find the largest open space.

3. Are family heirlooms nearby?

Paper airplanes are light, but they can still have enough force to knock something over or break it. Be careful!

Indoors, you can turn walls, ceilings, and furniture into part of your flight course. You can aim for the couch or try to reach the ceiling.

Places to Fly

No doubt you have a good idea of where not to fly a plane: museums, libraries, the principal's office, your grandparents' house.

Here are a few places where you can test your wings. You may need to ask permission for some locations.

- School yard
- Backyard
- Gym
- Hallway
- Park
- Baseball field
- Auditorium
- Cafeteria

The Nuts and Bolts of Folding

Every paper airplane is only as good as its folds. A good fold can overcome a poor throw, but even a perfect toss will not save a poorly folded plane. You can have the best design in the world, but with sloppy, soft creases, your plane will never soar. Making accurate, sharp creases may take a little more time, but you'll see better results.

First, start with a clean, smooth, hard surface. If you're folding your plane on your lunch bag or a sofa cushion, your plane will head straight for the trash bin.

Next, use good flying paper. The papers included in this book will make sharp folds and great flyers. Regular printer paper will work well, too. But don't waste your time with loose-leaf notebook paper!

Learn How to Read the Diagrams

For the planes you will fold in this book, edges and corners are your copilots. They're your guides to making the folds. In most cases, you will be lining up a corner with another corner, an edge with another edge. Or you'll be using your previous folds as your guidelines and making new folds to meet them. Keep your eyes on the edges as you make your folds.

Make crisp folds. Start with a "soft fold," testing where the edges line up. When you've found the perfect spot, use the back of your thumb to make a sharp crease.

Watch for bulges and bubbles, and flatten them as you fold. When you're done with a fold, run the side of a pencil or a craft stick over the whole area, pressing down hard.

For example, in the diagram below, you need to take the top left corner and bring it down to meet the center crease. The dotted line shows where your fold will be. Also, when you reach each step of the instructions, make sure to turn the folded paper to match the position of the shape in the diagram.

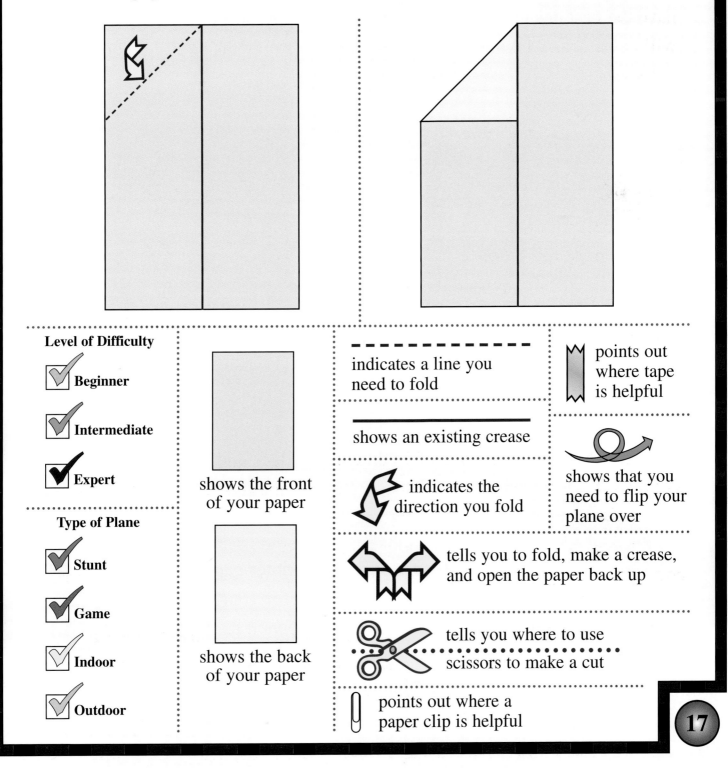

Level of Difficulty

☑ **Beginner**

☑ **Intermediate**

☑ **Expert**

Type of Plane

☑ **Stunt**

☑ **Game**

☑ **Indoor**

☑ **Outdoor**

shows the front of your paper

shows the back of your paper

– – – – – – – – indicates a line you need to fold

────── shows an existing crease

indicates the direction you fold

tells you to fold, make a crease, and open the paper back up

points out where tape is helpful

shows that you need to flip your plane over

tells you where to use scissors to make a cut

points out where a paper clip is helpful

Make It Even-Steven

It's all about symmetry—making both sides identical. For paper airplanes, whatever you do to one side, you need to do to the other. If one side is just a little bit off, you will notice that your plane does not fly straight.

So if you make a small mistake on one side, fix it—or make the same mistake on the other.

Even if some of your folds don't quite match up, you may find that your plane flies well. But the most important place to achieve symmetry on your plane is the wings. Focus on making them as even as possible.

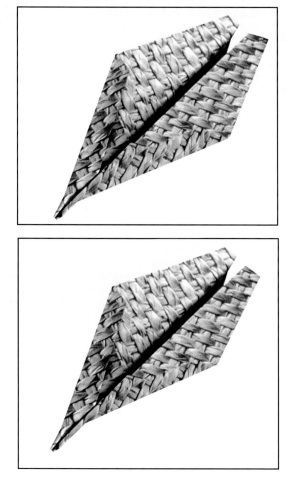

Look at these two models.
Which one will fly straight?

What You Need

Just a piece of paper! That's the beauty of paper airplanes—
you don't need a long supply list, a trip to the craft store, or safety gear.
But it's a good idea to keep a few simple items handy.

• Flight-ready plane paper or regular printer paper. Start with
printer paper and save the sheets in this book for your best models • Clear
plastic tape • Scissors • Craft stick, comb, or pencil to use for folding sharp
creases • Markers or colored pencils for decorating your plain-paper planes.
• Ruler • Paper clips

Launching Your Plane

Making a paper plane soar takes more than just winging it into the air. Once again, practice makes perfect. Here are a few tips for launching your plane.

1. Grip the plane.

Using whatever hand you write with, pinch the airplane body with your thumb and pointer finger. Generally, you want to pinch the plane near the center.

Pinching your fingers

Right way

Wrong way

2. Look around you.

Check your surroundings for little brothers and sisters, family heirlooms, and other hazards. Be especially careful with pointy-nosed models (see Traffic Control, page 14).

3. Launch a test toss.

Your first flight with a new plane is its test run. You don't want to hurl it like a baseball, or it will surely crash. Start out nice and easy. Hold the plane just in front of your shoulder. Gently push your hand forward and release.

4. Observe and correct.

Check your plane's individual tendencies. Does it veer to the right or left, or does it nose-dive? See Maintenance and Troubleshooting, page 20, to correct these bad habits.

5. Go for broke.

Once you've performed your test tosses and corrected for flight flaws, give it your all. Start by throwing your plane a little harder. In order for a plane to fly a long time, you need height. Aim as high as your surroundings will allow.

Each Plane
Requires a Unique Toss

- Every plane is different, and you'll need to experiment to find the best way to toss each one.

- The best spot to grip the plane is its center of gravity. Grip the plane loosely at various points along the body. The point where the plane balances is its center of gravity.

- Refer to the folding instructions for each plane for tips on launching.

- Experiment with the angle of your launch. Test the same plane with a downward launch, upward launch, and various angles in between. Different angles create different air flows.

Maintenance and Troubleshooting

You've folded your plane perfectly and given it an expert toss—and it still tanks. We've all been there! Before you toss it in the garbage, try a few tweaks that the pros use.

1. Check for flight damage.

After each flight, survey your plane. Pointy-nosed planes are especially susceptible to crumple damage. Other planes may need to be recreased, or the wings may need adjustment after a bumpy flight.

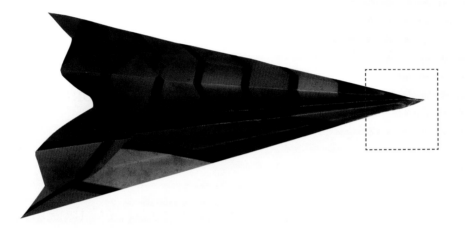

2. Check for symmetry.

Make sure each side is identical.
Tweak the folds so that both sides match as closely as possible.

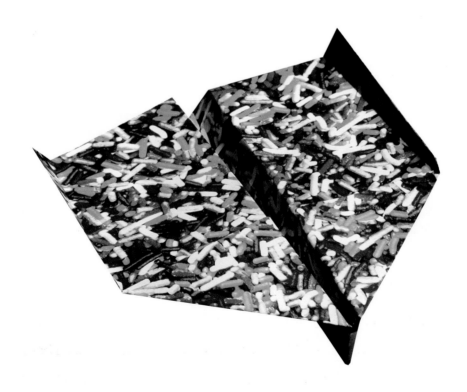

3. Adjust the wing angle.

The *dihedral* is the angle of the wings, as shown below. A slight V shape adds stability to the plane's flight. Some stunt planes work best without this structure. Experiment to see its effects.

Dihedral

4. Create elevators.

Elevators are little flaps added to the back of a plane's wings. Depending on how you crimp the wing, you can make your plane go up or down. If your plane is nose-diving, try adding up-elevators that make the plane go higher, as shown.

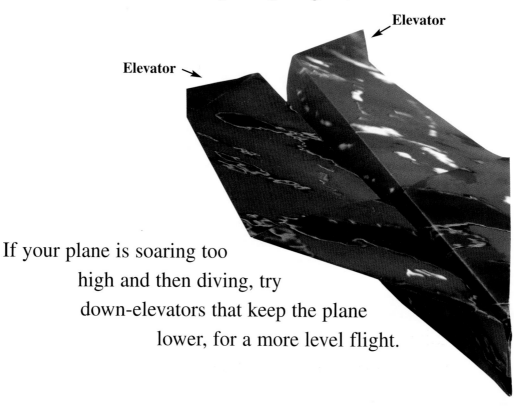

Elevator

Elevator

If your plane is soaring too high and then diving, try down-elevators that keep the plane lower, for a more level flight.

5. Create an aileron.

If you want to make your plane turn in a particular direction, create an *aileron*. An aileron is just like an elevator, but it's added toward the end of one wing. In this case, you do not want symmetry. Make just one aileron on the opposite wing of the direction you want the plane to turn.

Aileron →

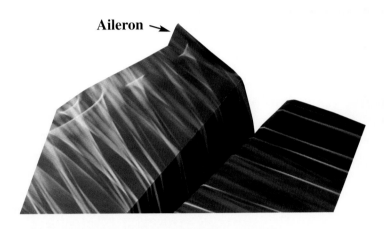

6. Adjust the rudder.

If your plane tends toward one side, you may also need to adjust the rudder, if your plane has one. If your plane is veering to the left, bend your rudder slightly to the right. If it's heading toward the right, bend the rudder to the left.

Rudder

Rudder

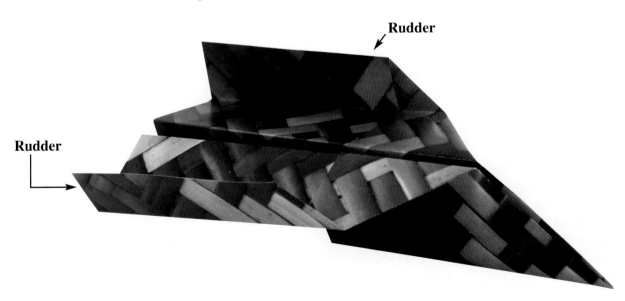

If all these adjustments fail, you can always consider your plane a stunt plane (see Stunt Planes, page 24).

Create Your Own Plane

Once you've successfully flown the planes in this book, you're ready to reach for the sky. You understand the principles of flight and how to fold well, launch, and make corrections. It's time to design your own ideal plane. Keep the following tips in mind:

- Start with a center fold.
- Remember that symmetry is key! Whatever you do to one side, do to the other.
- Create a nose with some bulk. The front needs to be heavier than the back.
- Keep in mind, as you create wings, that extra creases can add stability.
- Test and adjust. Keep a record in the Daily Flight Records section (page 65).
- Decorate and name your plane.

Stunt Planes

With a few secret tips, you can make your plane flip, dive, and fly in circles. These tricks have a big payoff, and they're easy to do. The secret is in the elevators and the toss.

Loop-the-Loop

1. Start with the appropriate plane. We recommend the Flipper and the Bat as great stunt planes.
2. Add up-elevators. Bend them almost straight up.
3. Holding the plane behind your shoulder, launch it straight up with a gentle vertical toss.
4. Watch your plane rise, flip over, dive down, and recover!

Dive

1. Add extreme up-elevators to your plane.
2. From a high point (standing on a chair, for example), launch the plane straight downward.
3. Just when you think it's going to hit the floor, it should swoop up and level off.
4. Now try launching the plane with the nose pointing up. Drop the plane, and watch it perform a *tail slide*. It should do a backflip.

Boomerang

1. Add extreme up-elevators.
2. Hold the plane near your shoulder at an angle. Tilt the plane so that the right wing is lower than the left.
3. Now throw the plane straight ahead, as level as you can. The plane should make a circle.
4. If the plane doesn't boomerang back to you, try creating a rudder on the right side (see page 23).

- [x] Beginner
- [x] Stunt
- [x] Indoor
- [x] Outdoor

The Starling

This plane can glide and dip like a bird in a breeze.

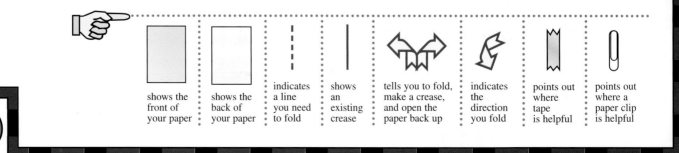

Experiment with throwing it at different angles. Can you make it twirl?

shows the front of your paper	shows the back of your paper	indicates a line you need to fold	shows an existing crease	tells you to fold, make a crease, and open the paper back up	indicates the direction you fold	points out where tape is helpful	points out where a paper clip is helpful

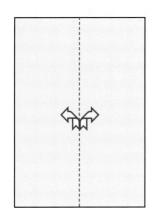 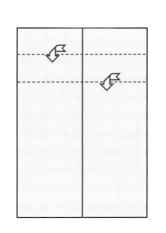 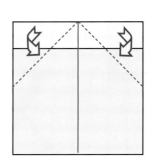

Step 1. Fold paper in half lengthwise. Unfold, leaving a center crease.

Step 2. Fold down the top edge about 1¾". The center crease should line up on top of itself. Make a sharp crease. Repeat this one more time so that you have made two 1¾" folds. Make a sharp crease. Press down firmly.

Step 3. Fold each corner down so that the top edge lies along the center crease. Recrease all folds well.

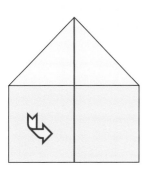

Step 4. Fold in half.

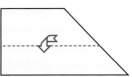

Step 5. Fold one wing down about 2" from the center crease. Repeat on the other wing. Check for symmetry.

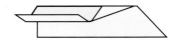 

Step 6. Fold the rudder up about 1" from the bottom edge. Repeat on the other wing. Check for symmetry.

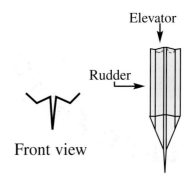

Elevator

Rudder

Front view

☞ Tips:

- Refold your center crease each time you fold down from the top.
- Check for dents after each flight and repair as needed.
- For added stability, place a piece of tape on the nose.
- Place a paper clip near the front of the plane for added speed.

☑ **Beginner**

☑ **Stunt**

☑ **Indoor**

☑ **Outdoor**

The X5 Astrolite

This is a sturdy, dependable flyer—indoors and out. With its blunt nose, it's ready to go the distance.

shows the front of your paper	shows the back of your paper	indicates a line you need to fold	shows an existing crease	tells you to fold, make a crease, and open the paper back up	indicates the direction you fold	points out where tape is helpful

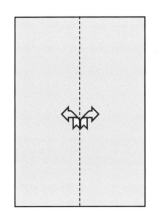

Step 1. Fold paper in half lengthwise. Unfold, leaving a center crease.

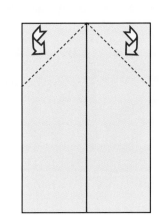

Step 2. Fold the top two corners down so that the top edges lie along the center crease. Press hard on the folds.

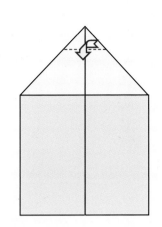

Step 3. Fold the top down about 1¾". The center crease should line up on top of itself. Make a sharp crease.

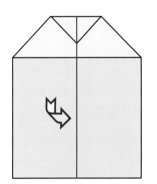

Step 4. Fold in half lengthwise along the center crease. Make a sharp crease.

top left edge

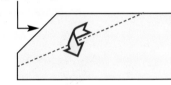

Step 5. Fold the top wing down at the angle shown. The top left edge should line up along the bottom. Match this fold to make the other wing.

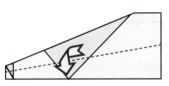

Step 6. Fold this layer at the angle shown so that the top edge lies along the bottom. Check that your plane is symmetrical. Repeat on the other wing. Press firmly.

☞ Tips:

- Place a small piece of tape where shown and wrap it around the other side.
- To launch, hold the plane between the nose and the spot where the tape is placed.
- Flare out the back of the wings.
- Launch with an upward throw. Your force will determine the plane's distance.

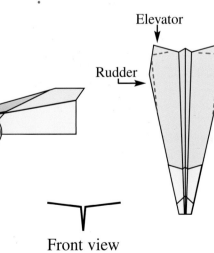

Elevator

Rudder

Front view

The Shark

The Shark likes to keep moving, and its dorsal fin will set the course. Remember to keep the Shark's nose up. This simple plane will give you great results.

shows the front of your paper

shows the back of your paper

indicates a line you need to fold

indicates the direction you fold

points out where a paper clip is helpful

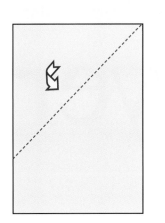 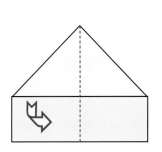 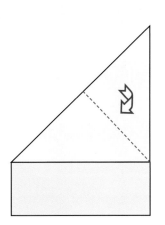

Step 1. Fold the paper's top left corner so that the top edge and right edge line up.

Step 2. Fold over the top right corner, lining up the edges. Press the folds firmly.

Step 3. Fold in half left to right. Press the folds again.

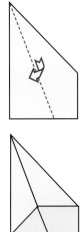 

Step 5. Repeat step 4 on the other wing. Check for symmetry, and press firmly on the creases.

Step 4. Fold the top wing over to make the edges line up.

Elevator

Rudder

☞Tips:

- This plane likes a soft, upward launch.
- Moving or curling the large dorsal-fin rudder to the left or right will change the flight direction.
- Add a paper clip near the nose for added speed.
- Check for dents after each flight and repair as needed.

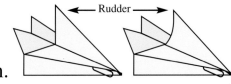

Rudder

The Ace Flyer

The Ace Flyer is the plane for you when you need speed and accuracy.

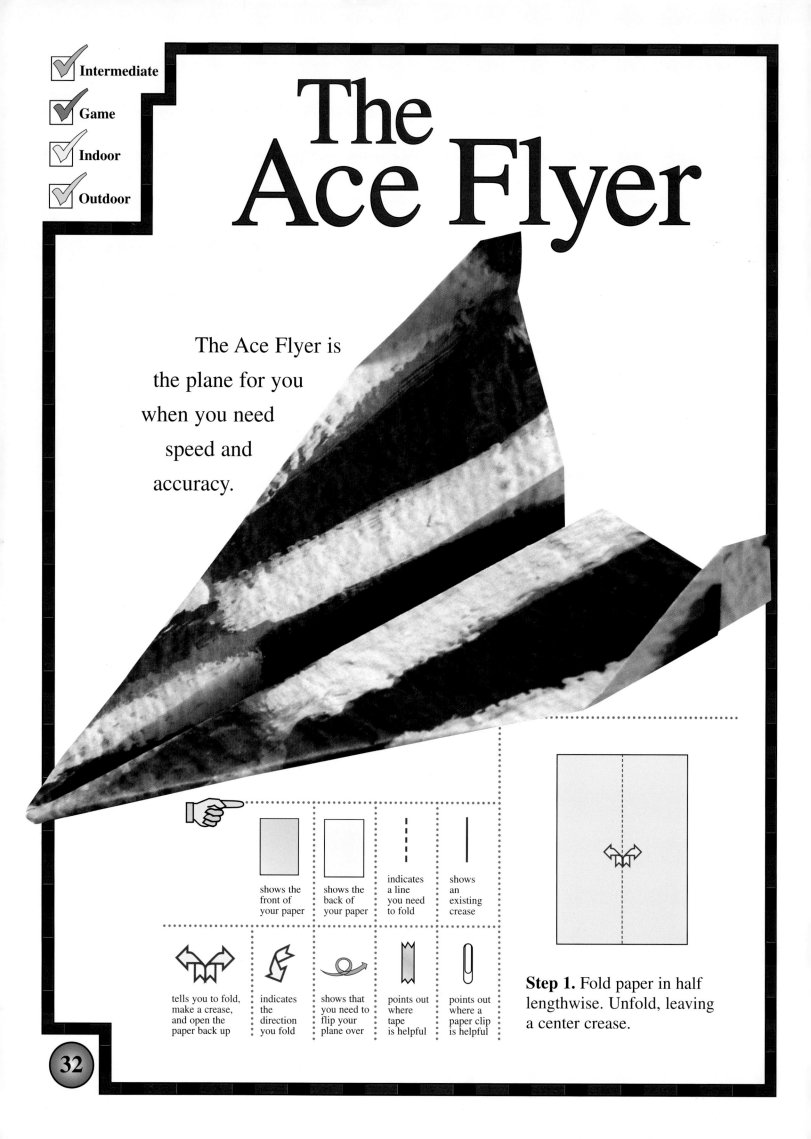

shows the front of your paper	shows the back of your paper	indicates a line you need to fold	shows an existing crease
tells you to fold, make a crease, and open the paper back up	indicates the direction you fold	shows that you need to flip your plane over	points out where tape is helpful	points out where a paper clip is helpful

Step 1. Fold paper in half lengthwise. Unfold, leaving a center crease.

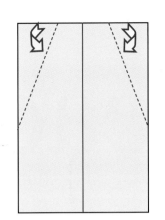

Step 2. Fold the top two corners in to meet at the center crease about 1½" from the top.

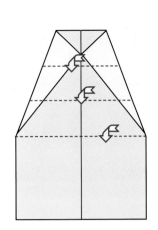

Step 3. Fold down the top edge about 2¼". The center crease should line up on top of itself. Fold down two more times so that you have made three 2¼" folds.

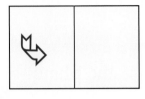

Step 4. Your paper should look like this. Now turn it over.

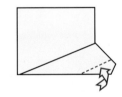

Step 5. Fold in half along the center crease.

Step 6. Fold the top wing down so that the left edge lies along the bottom.

Step 7. Fold down again, pressing firmly. Make sure the edges line up.

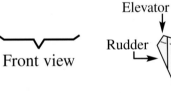

Step 8. Create a rudder by folding the wing tip up as shown. Match these folds to make the other wing. Check for symmetry.

Elevator

Rudder

Front view

☞ Tips:

- For added stability, place a small piece of tape where shown and wrap it around the other side.
- For additional speed, place a paper clip near the front of the plane.
- This plane needs a forceful, upward launch.
- Check for dents after each flight and repair as needed.

The Arrowhead

This is a jumbo jet. At 12½", the Arrowhead is the longest plane when made with the flight-ready plane paper.

It's a great plane for the Launch-and-Land Games poster.

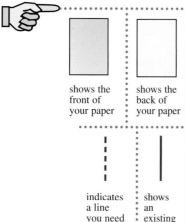

shows the front of your paper	shows the back of your paper

indicates a line you need to fold	shows an existing crease	tells you to fold, make a crease, and open the paper back up	indicates the direction you fold

Step 1. Fold paper in half lengthwise. Unfold, leaving a center crease.

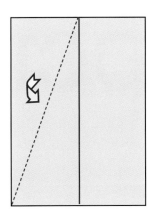

Step 2. Use a ruler to draw a line that connects the lower left corner with the center top. Make a sharp crease along the line.

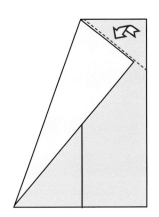

Step 3. Fold the upper right corner along the new edge you created as shown. Make a sharp crease.

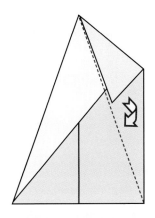

Step 4. Make a soft fold along a fold line that connects the lower right corner with the center top. When you have found the correct angle, make a sharp crease.

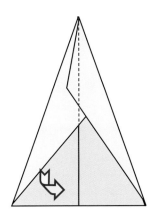

Step 5. Fold the plane in half lengthwise so the edges line up. Check for symmetry. Make crisp creases.

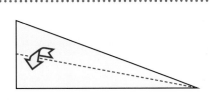

Step 6. Fold the wing down so that the edges line up. Make a sharp crease. Repeat on the other wing. Check symmetry.

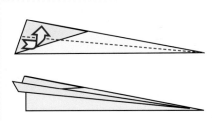

Step 7. Fold the rudder up so that the edges line up. Make a sharp crease. Repeat on the other wing. Check symmetry.

Step 8. Make a soft triangle fold as shown, then tuck the section into the back of the plane. Check for symmetry, and press hard on all folds.

 Tips:

- Hold your plane at the midpoint and launch with a gentle, smooth toss.
- Check for dents after each flight and repair as needed.

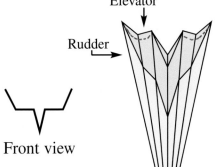

Elevator

Rudder

Front view

The Flipper

With a light, upward throw,
the Flipper will fly smoothly for a long way.
With a forceful throw,
the Flipper will soar,
flip over, and fly
upside down.

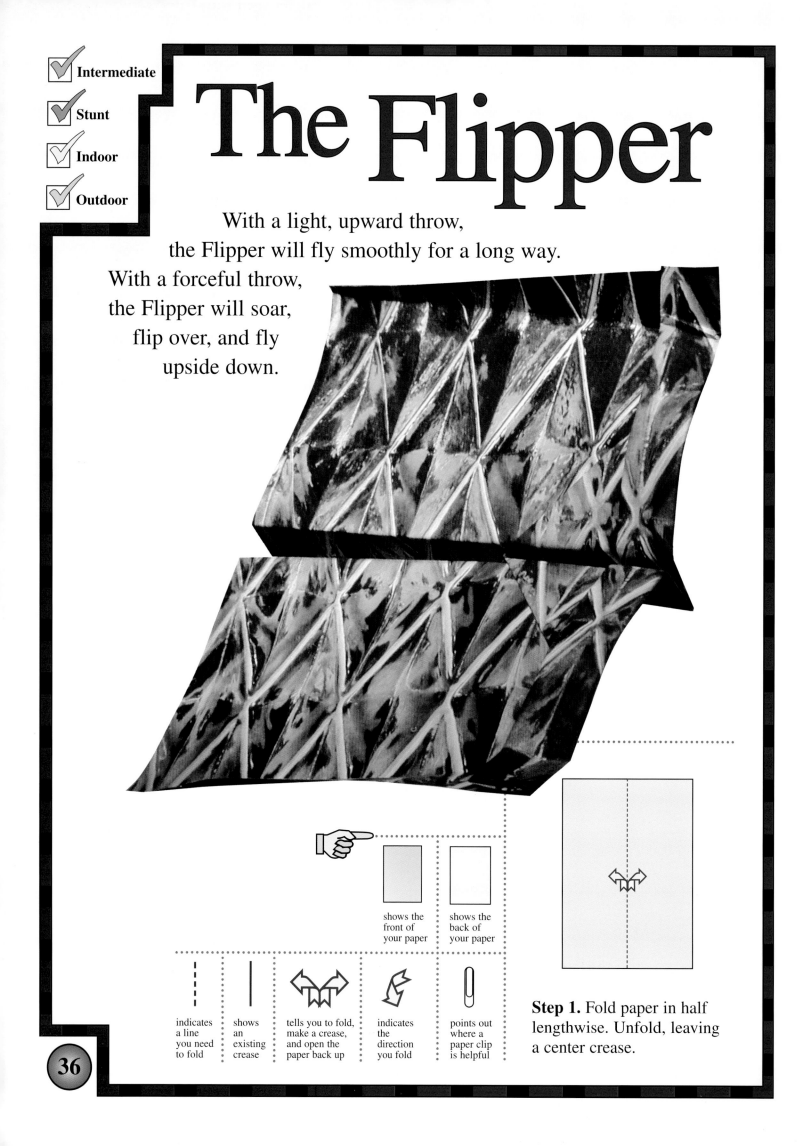

shows the front of your paper	shows the back of your paper

indicates a line you need to fold	shows an existing crease	tells you to fold, make a crease, and open the paper back up	indicates the direction you fold	points out where a paper clip is helpful

Step 1. Fold paper in half lengthwise. Unfold, leaving a center crease.

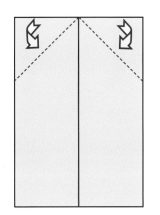

Step 2. Fold the top two corners down so that the top edges lie along the center crease.

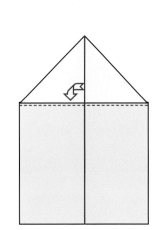

Step 3. Fold down the top. The center crease should line up on top of itself. Make a sharp crease.

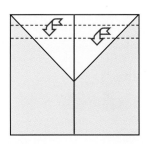

Step 4. Fold down the top edge about ¾". The center crease should line up on top of itself. Fold down one more time so that you have made two ¾" folds. Press firmly.

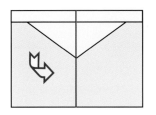

Step 5. Fold in half. Press firmly.

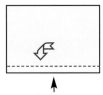

center crease

Step 6. Fold the top wing down about ¾" from the center crease. Repeat on the other wing. Press down firmly.

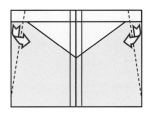

Step 7. Fold the wing tips up as shown to create the rudders.

Front view

Elevator

Rudder

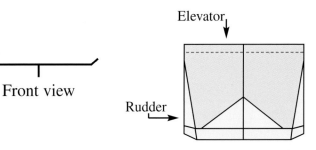

🖝 Tips:

- Launch with a light, upward throw.
- For distance and speed when flying outside,  add a paper clip as shown. Adjust rudders as needed.
- If your Flipper flies too high, add down-elevators.

The Dart

Toss this plane hard
and it really zooms
and spins like a dart.

Try it with the
Launch-and-Land
Games poster.

shows the front of your paper	shows the back of your paper	indicates a line you need to fold	shows an existing crease
tells you to fold, make a crease, and open the paper back up	indicates the direction you fold	points out where a paper clip is helpful	

Step 1. Fold paper in half lengthwise. Unfold, leaving a center crease.

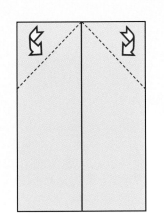

Step 2. Fold the top two corners down so that the top edges lie along the center crease.

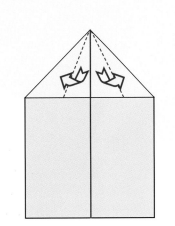

Step 3. Fold the inner corners out so that the edges line up along the outside. Crease sharply.

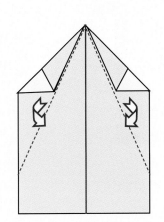

Step 4. Fold the sides in so that the edges lie along the center crease.

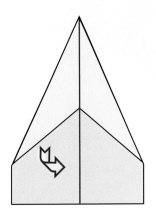

Step 5. Fold in half lengthwise along the center crease. Make a sharp crease.

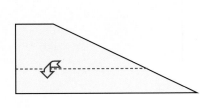

Step 6. Fold the wing down about 1½" from the center crease. Press firmly. Repeat on the other wing. Check for symmetry.

Step 7. Fold the rudder up as shown. Repeat on the other wing.

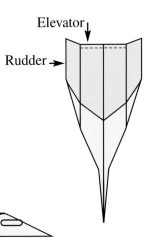

Elevator

Rudder →

Front view

☞ Tips:

- Add a paper clip for greater speed.

- Give a strong, smooth, upward toss to launch.

- Hold the plane near the middle.

- Open the plane and flare out the back of the wings.

- Check for dents after each flight and repair as needed.

- ☑ **Intermediate**
- ☑ **Game**
- ☑ **Indoor**
- ☑ **Outdoor**

The Condor is built for speed and distance. Fly it indoors and outdoors, or use it for the Launch-and-Land Games poster.

The Condor

shows the front of your paper	shows the back of your paper	┊ indicates a line you need to fold	│ shows an existing crease

 tells you to fold, make a crease, and open the paper back up

indicates the direction you fold

points out where tape is helpful

Step 1. Fold paper in half lengthwise. Unfold, leaving a center crease.

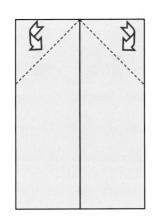

Step 2. Fold the top two corners down so that the top edges lie along the center crease.

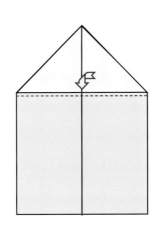

Step 3. Fold the top down along the bottom edge of the large triangle you just made so that the top point lines up with the center crease.

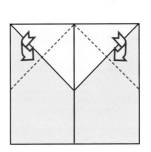

Step 4. Fold the top two corners down again so that the top edges line up along the center crease. Press down hard and crease well.

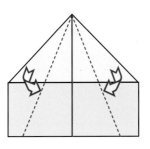

Step 5. Fold the sides in so that the edges line up along the center crease. Press firmly.

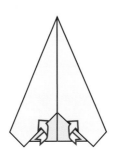

Step 6. Fold in half lengthwise along the center crease.

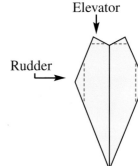

Step 7. Holding the center crease, open the wings. Check for symmetry.

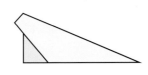

Front view

Elevator

Rudder

 Tips:

• This plane needs a strong, smooth, upward toss.

• For additional stability, place a small piece of tape where shown and wrap it around the other side.

• Check for dents after each flight and repair as needed.

The Comet

The Comet can do it all.
Keep the nose up, and it will
fly as far as you push it!

shows the
front of
your paper

shows the
back of
your paper

indicates
a line
you need
to fold

shows
an
existing
crease

tells you to fold,
make a crease,
and open the
paper back up

indicates
the
direction
you fold

Step 1. Fold paper in half
lengthwise. Unfold, leaving
a center crease.

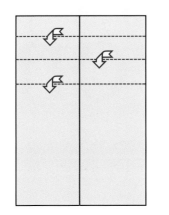

Step 2. Fold down the top edge about 1¾". The center crease should line up on top of itself. Fold down two more times so that you have made three 1¾" folds.

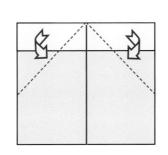

Step 3. Fold the top two corners down so that the top edges lie along the center crease. Press down hard.

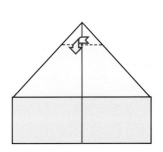

Step 4. Fold down the top point about 1¼". The center crease should line up on top of itself. Make a sharp crease and press firmly.

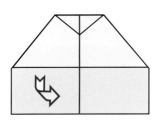

Step 5. Fold in half along the center crease. Press firmly.

top left edge

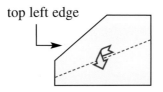

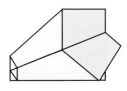

Step 6. Fold the top wing down at the angle shown. The top left edge should line up with the bottom. Match this fold to make the other wing.

Elevator

Rudder

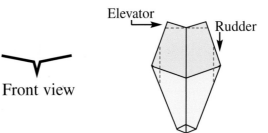

Front view

👉 Tips:

• Launch with a light, upward throw.

• This plane is bulky, so you must check and press creases firmly.

• Add a slight upward curl to the elevators for a long flight.

The Falcon

This plane is best flown in wide-open spaces, where it can glide and twirl.

shows the front of your paper	shows the back of your paper	indicates a line you need to fold	shows an existing crease	tells you to fold, make a crease, and open the paper back up	indicates the direction you fold	shows that you need to flip your plane over	points out where tape is helpful

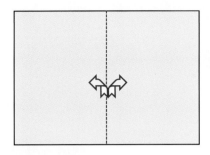

Step 1. Start with your paper turned sideways as shown. Then fold in half widthwise. Unfold, leaving a center crease.

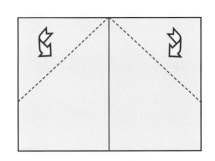

Step 2. Fold the top two corners down so that the top edges lie along the center crease. Press down firmly.

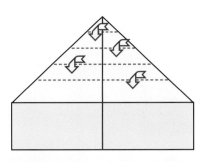

Step 3. Fold the top down about 1". The center crease should line up on top of itself. Repeat this same fold three more times so that you have made four 1" folds. Press down firmly.

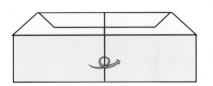

Step 4. Your paper should look like this. Now turn it over.

Step 5. Fold in half along the center crease. Press hard and crease well.

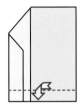

Step 6. Fold the top wing down about ¾" from the center crease. Repeat on the other wing. Check for symmetry. Press firmly.

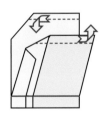

Step 7. Fold rudders up as shown.

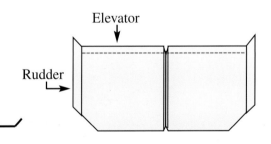

Elevator

Rudder

Front view

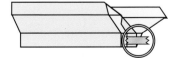

☞ Tips:

- Place a small piece of tape where shown and wrap it around the other side for stability.
- Give this plane a straight, firm, upward toss.
- Test your plane and adjust as needed.

☑ **Intermediate**

☑ **Stunt**

☑ **Indoor**

☑ **Outdoor**

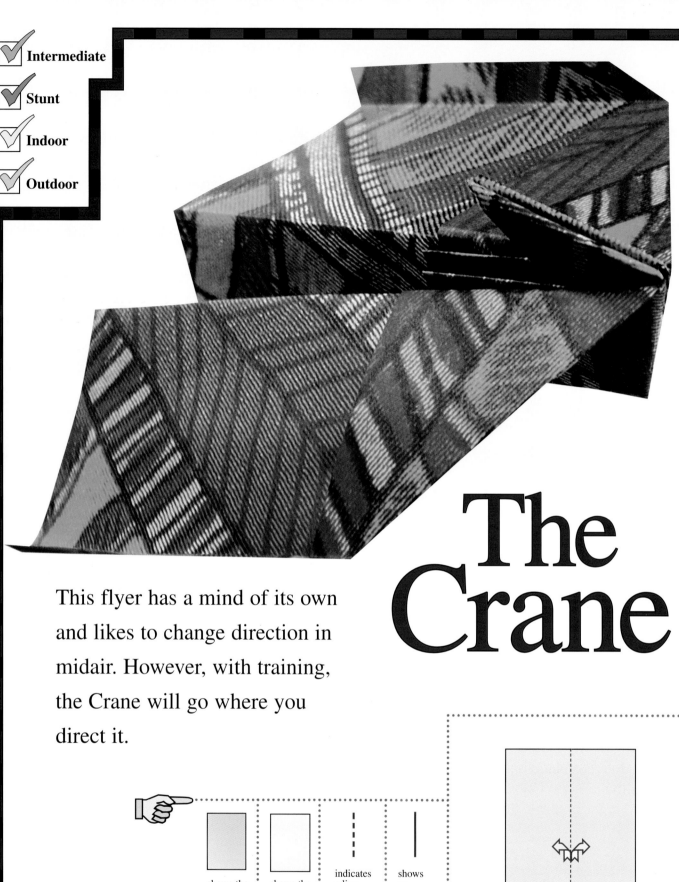

The Crane

This flyer has a mind of its own and likes to change direction in midair. However, with training, the Crane will go where you direct it.

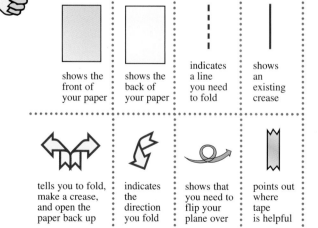

shows the front of your paper	shows the back of your paper	indicates a line you need to fold	shows an existing crease
tells you to fold, make a crease, and open the paper back up	indicates the direction you fold	shows that you need to flip your plane over	points out where tape is helpful

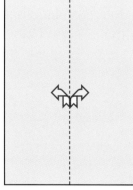

Step 1. Fold paper in half lengthwise. Unfold, leaving a center crease.

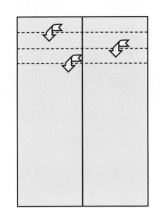

Step 2. Fold down the top edge about 1". The center crease should line up on top of itself. Make a sharp crease. Repeat this two more times so that you have made three 1" folds.

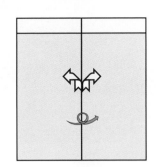

Step 3. Recrease through the center, making sure the thicker folded strips are all sharply creased. Press firmly and then turn the paper over.

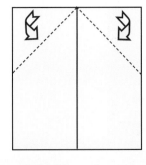

Step 4. Fold each corner down so that the top edges lie along the center crease. Press firmly on all folds.

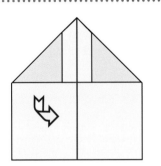

Step 5. Fold in half.

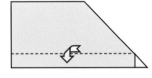

Step 6. Fold the wing down about 1" from the center crease. Repeat to make the other wing. Check for symmetry, press firmly, and then unfold both wings.

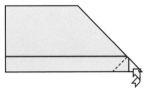

Step 7. Fold the tip upward at the angle shown, forming a triangle. Unfold, and then make the same fold and crease on the other side.

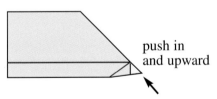

push in and upward

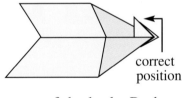

correct position

Step 8. Hold the plane lightly in the center of the body. Push in the bottom crease below the triangle so that the triangle lifts and sticks up inside the plane. Fold down the wings again.

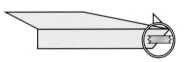

Step 9. Place a small piece of tape where shown and wrap it around the other side.

☞Tips:

- Recrease the center after each fold is made.
- Hold the plane near the front to launch, using a smooth, upward throw.
- If the plane flies too high, add down-elevators.
- Flare the dihedral for a smooth flight.

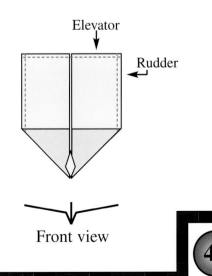

Elevator

Rudder

Front view

47

- [x] **Intermediate**
- [x] **Game**
- [x] **Indoor**
- [x] **Outdoor**

This faceted plane is a strong flyer.

The Diamond

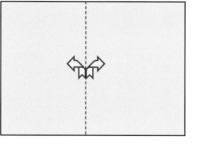

shows the front of your paper	shows the back of your paper

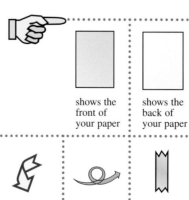

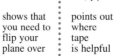

indicates a line you need to fold	shows an existing crease	tells you to fold, make a crease, and open the paper back up	indicates the direction you fold	shows that you need to flip your plane over	points out where tape is helpful

Step 1. Start with your paper turned sideways as shown. Then fold in half widthwise. Unfold, leaving a center crease.

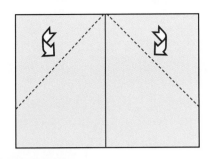

Step 2. Fold the top two corners down so that the top edges lie along the center crease. Press these folds well.

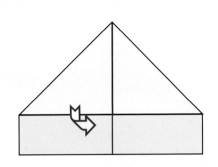

Step 3. Fold in half along the center crease line. Check for symmetry. Press firmly.

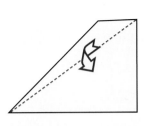

Step 4. Fold the top layer down as shown, along a line from the bottom left corner to the top right. Press firmly.

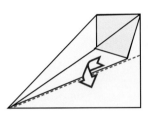

Step 5. Fold over again using the edge of your previous fold as a guide. Press firmly.

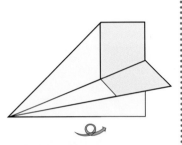

Step 6. Your paper should look like this. Now turn it over.

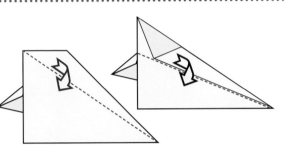

Step 7. Match the folds from steps 4 and 5 to make the other wing. Check for symmetry. Press firmly.

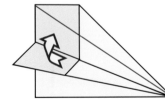

Step 8. Open the wings, unfolding them as shown in step 9.

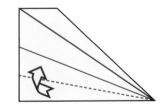 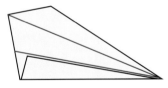

Step 9. Fold up the bottom edge so it lines up with the crease line. Press firmly.

☞ Tips:

- Hold the plane near the front to launch, and give a light, upward throw.
- Open the plane and flare out the back of the wings slightly.
- Check for dents after each flight and repair as needed.
- For greater stability, add a piece of tape to the fold in step 9.

Elevator

Front view

Rudder →

This model can do flips
and loops, and it glides
to Earth like a
feather. It flies
great indoors
and outdoors.

The Feather

shows the front of your paper

shows the back of your paper

indicates a line you need to fold

shows an existing crease

tells you to fold, make a crease, and open the paper back up

indicates the direction you fold

Step 1. Fold paper in half lengthwise. Unfold, leaving a center crease.

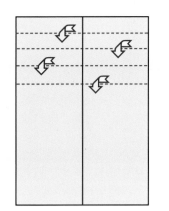

Step 2. Fold down the top edge about 1". The center crease should line up on top of itself. Repeat this same fold three more times so that you have made four 1" folds. Crease well and press down hard.

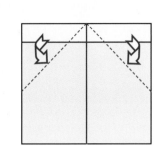

Step 3. Fold the top two corners down so that the top edge lies near the center crease. Crease these folds well.

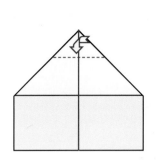

Step 4. Fold down the top point about 1¾". The center crease should line up on top of itself. Make a sharp crease. Press firmly.

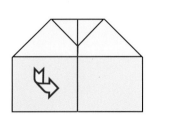

Step 5. Fold in half lengthwise along the center crease.

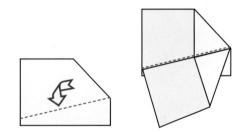

Step 6. Fold the wing down along a crease line that is about 1¾" (on the right) and about ½" (on the left) from the center crease. Match this fold to make the other wing. Check for symmetry. Press creases firmly.

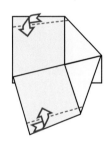

Step 7. Fold the rudders up as shown.

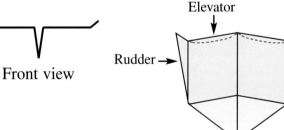

Front view

Elevator

Rudder →

 Tips:

• Hold the plane near the front to launch, and give it a smooth, moderate, upward throw.

• Check for dents after each flight and repair as needed.

51

☑ **Expert**
☑ **Indoor**
☑ **Outdoor**

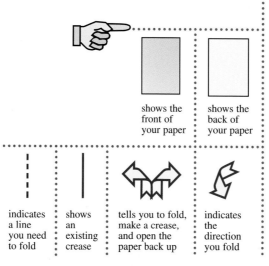

The Hawk

Launch this glider upward,
toward the sky,
and watch it fly.

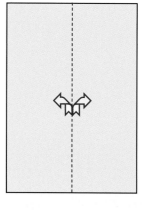

shows the front of your paper	shows the back of your paper

indicates a line you need to fold	shows an existing crease	tells you to fold, make a crease, and open the paper back up	indicates the direction you fold

Step 1. Fold paper in half lengthwise. Unfold, leaving a center crease.

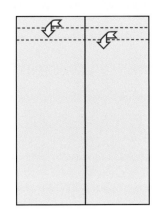

Step 2. Fold the top edge down about ¾". The center crease should line up on top of itself. Repeat this same fold one more time so that you have made two ¾" folds. Crease well and press down hard.

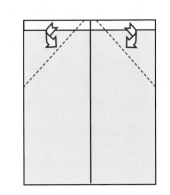

Step 3. Fold the top two corners down so that the top edges lie parallel to the center fold and ¼" away from it. Crease folds well.

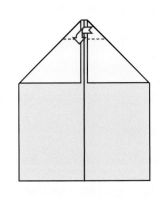

Step 4. Fold the top down about 1½". The center crease should line up on top of itself. Crease well and press down hard.

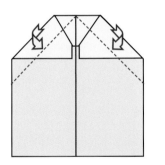

Step 5. Fold the top two corners down again so the top edges meet on either side of the center crease. Crease these folds well.

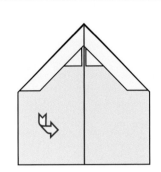

Step 6. Fold in half lengthwise along the center crease. Check for symmetry.

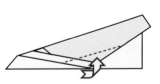

Step 8. Open the plane and fold the rudders straight up.

top left corner

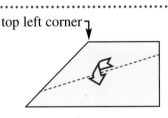

Step 7. Soft-fold the wing down as you find the correct angle. The front of the wing starts right above the thick tip, and the top left corner touches the bottom edge.

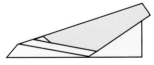

When you've found the correct angle, make a crisp fold. Match this fold to make the other wing. Check for symmetry.

 Tips:

- Launch with a light, upward toss with wings level to the ground.
- Check for dents after each flight and repair as needed.
- Test your plane, and add up-elevators to make it really climb!

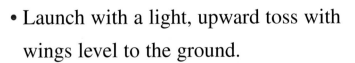

Front view

Elevator

Rudder

The Bat

An all-around great flyer, the Bat soars
and glides. With six elevators,
the Bat is flight-ready
to practice stunts.

shows the front of your paper

shows the back of your paper

indicates a line you need to fold

shows an existing crease

indicates the direction you fold

tells you where to use scissors to make a cut

Step 1. Start with your paper turned sideways as shown. Then fold in half widthwise.

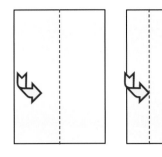 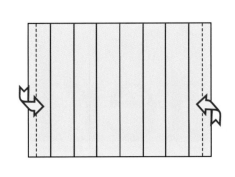

Step 2. Fold the paper in half again and then in half once more. Press down firmly.

Step 3. Unfold the paper. Fold in about ½" from either end. These will become your rudders.

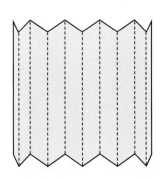

Step 4. Pinch the center fold together. Starting with the creases on either side of the center, fold the paper in the opposite direction of the original folds so the paper is folded accordion-style. The ends and center should be folded in the same direction. Press creases well.

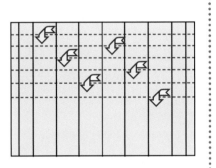

Step 5. Unfold the paper. Fold the top down about ¾". Fold so that the crease lines match up. Repeat this same fold five more times so that you have made six ¾" folds. Crease well and press down hard.

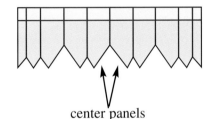

center panels

Step 6. Pinch together the two center panels of the plane.

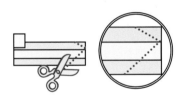

Step 7. Accordion-fold your plane again and firmly recrease all folds, pressing down hard. With your plane folded, press firmly again and cut as shown.

Elevator

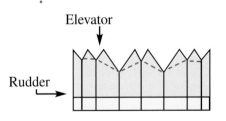

Rudder

Front view

Tips:

• This plane has six available elevators.

• Hold the plane in the front under the six folds.

• Launch with a level, smooth toss.

• Experiment by cutting different angles in the back.

55

The Butterfly

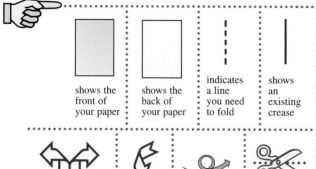

The Butterfly is ready to go the distance. With enough of an upward push, the Butterfly will travel far.

shows the front of your paper	shows the back of your paper	indicates a line you need to fold	shows an existing crease
tells you to fold, make a crease, and open the paper back up	indicates the direction you fold	shows that you need to flip your plane over	tells you where to use scissors to make a cut

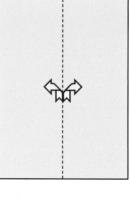

Step 1. Fold paper in half lengthwise. Unfold, leaving a center crease.

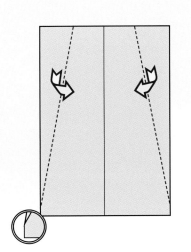

Step 2. Fold the top two corners in to meet at the center crease.

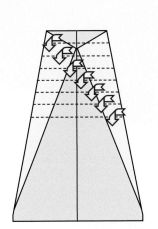

Step 3. Fold down the top edge about ¾". The center crease should line up on top of itself. Fold down six more times so that you have made seven ¾" folds.

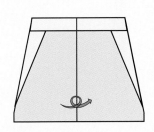

Step 4. Your paper should look like this. Now turn it over.

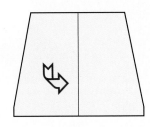

Step 5. Fold it in half along the center crease.

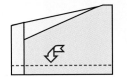

Step 6. Fold the top wing down about ½" from the center crease. Repeat on the other wing. Check for symmetry. Crease well.

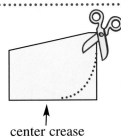

center crease

Step 7. With the center crease at the bottom, make a curved cut as shown. You can use the edge of a plate to outline your curve before you cut. Cut carefully along the line.

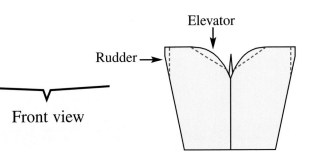

Elevator

Rudder →

Front view

☞ Tips:

- Hold your plane in front to launch.
- Indoors, give a gentle, smooth toss.
- Outdoors, the Butterfly can take your strongest toss!
- Remember to aim high.
- For step 7, experiment by cutting other shapes from this plane. Test your planes. How did the shapes affect their flight?

✔ **Expert**

✔ **Indoor**

✔ **Outdoor**

The graceful

curved wing

on this flyer

catches

the wind.

The Sea Gull

shows the front of your paper	shows the back of your paper	indicates a line you need to fold	shows an existing crease

tells you to fold, make a crease, and open the paper back up	indicates the direction you fold

Step 1. Start with your paper turned sideways as shown. Then fold in half widthwise. Unfold, leaving a center crease.

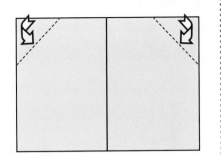

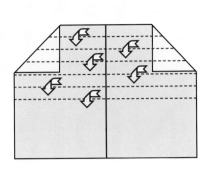

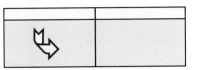

Step 2. Fold the top two corners in about 3" from the top edge. Crease these folds well.

Step 3. Fold down the top edge about ¾". The center crease should line up on top of itself. Repeat this same fold five more times so that you have made six ¾" folds. Crease well and press down hard.

Step 4. Fold in half along the center crease. Check for symmetry. Press down hard.

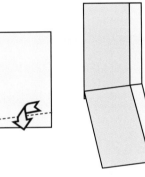

Step 5. With the folded strip on your right, fold down the wing along a crease line that is about 1" (on the right) and about ½" (on the left) from the center crease. Match this fold to make the other wing. Check for symmetry.

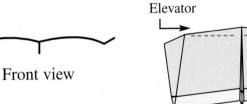

Step 6. Soft-fold rudders along the crease lines as shown. Check for symmetry.

Step 7. With two fingers above and your thumb beneath each wing, gently curve both wings as shown.

Front view

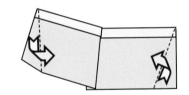

Elevator   Rudder

👉 Tips:

• This plane can loop and glide.

• Hold the plane near the front to launch, and give a strong, upward throw.

BULL'S-EYE LANDING

Flying paper airplanes can be a competitive sport. You can see whose plane goes the farthest or the fastest. With this pullout poster (see inside the back cover of this book), you can also compete for accuracy.

Players: 1 to 10

Materials Needed:
- Game poster
- Paper airplanes (1 per player)
- Paper and pen for scoring

Where to Play:
- Indoors or outdoors—anywhere with a flat space and plenty of room

How to Play:
- Each player should fold his or her own plane, using our models and paper or those created by each player.
- Lay the poster on a flat surface with the bull's-eye facing up.
- Mark a spot approximately 10 feet from the center of the poster.
- The first player launches his or her plane, aiming for the center of the bull's-eye.

- Watch carefully to see where the nose of the plane lands. Record that player's score.
- Repeat with all players.
- The first player to reach a score of 100 wins.
- Any player whose plane lands in the center is an instant winner.

Variations and Tips

- Let younger players stand closer to the target when they launch their planes.
- Launch all planes at the same time and try to avoid collisions.
- Give extra points for stunt landings.

MARS EXPLORATION

Send your own unmanned probe to explore Mars! You can use the pullout poster to play the Mars Exploration game with your friends. (See inside the back cover of this book.)

Players: 1 to 10

Materials Needed:
- Game poster
- Paper airplanes (1 per player)
- Paper and pen for scoring

Where to Play:
- Indoors or outdoors—anywhere with a flat space and plenty of room

How to Play:
- Each player should fold his or her own plane, using our models and paper or those created by each player.
- Lay the poster on a flat surface with Mars facing up.
- Mark a spot approximately 10 feet from the center of the poster.
- The first player launches his or her plane, aiming for a section on the surface of Mars.
- Watch carefully to see where the nose of the plane lands.
- If you land on a section with an *M*, *A*, *R*, or *S*, you have won that letter. Your goal is to collect the letters needed to spell MARS. If you land on a star, you may choose any letter you need. If you land on a plus sign, you get an extra toss. If you land on a triangle space, you lose a turn.
- Repeat with all players.
- The first player to collect the letters needed to spell MARS is the winner.

Highlights® Mars Exploration

If you land on a

 You can choose any letter you need!

You get an extra toss.

Sorry, you lose a turn.

DAILY FLIGHT RECORDS

Like all pilots, you'll need to keep a record of your flights. That way you'll know which planes performed well under various circumstances. Next time you fold the same plane, you can refer to your log. And you can keep track of your own personal records.

DIPLOMA
and
ACE-FLYER PILOT'S LICENSE

Congratulations! You've graduated from Highlights Flight School with sky-high honors! (Turn to page 67.) Fill out the diploma and display it with your best models.

You've earned your wings! Now that you've logged dozens of hours in Highlights Flight School and launched scores of planes, you're ready to fly solo. Cut out your Ace-Flyer Pilot's License. Don't forget to add your photo for identification. (See page 67.)

★ Daily Flight Records ★

FLIGHT RECORD

Date and Name of Model Paper Plane
Distance and Flying Time
Weather Conditions
Flying Remarks
Flying Adjustments

FLIGHT RECORD

Date and Name of Model Paper Plane
Distance and Flying Time
Weather Conditions
Flying Remarks
Flying Adjustments

FLIGHT RECORD

Date and Name of Model Paper Plane
Distance and Flying Time
Weather Conditions
Flying Remarks
Flying Adjustments

FLIGHT RECORD

Date and Name of Model Paper Plane
Distance and Flying Time
Weather Conditions
Flying Remarks
Flying Adjustments

FLIGHT RECORD

Date and Name of Model Paper Plane
Distance and Flying Time
Weather Conditions
Flying Remarks
Flying Adjustments

★ Daily Flight Records ★

FLIGHT RECORD

Date and Name of Model Paper Plane

Distance and Flying Time

Weather Conditions

Flying Remarks

Flying Adjustments

FLIGHT RECORD

Date and Name of Model Paper Plane

Distance and Flying Time

Weather Conditions

Flying Remarks

Flying Adjustments

FLIGHT RECORD

Date and Name of Model Paper Plane

Distance and Flying Time

Weather Conditions

Flying Remarks

Flying Adjustments

FLIGHT RECORD

Date and Name of Model Paper Plane

Distance and Flying Time

Weather Conditions

Flying Remarks

Flying Adjustments

FLIGHT RECORD

Date and Name of Model Paper Plane

Distance and Flying Time

Weather Conditions

Flying Remarks

Flying Adjustments

To remove, pull firmly along perforated lines.

Highlights® ⊕ Flight School
Graduation
Diploma

presented to

_____

for excellence in folding and launching
the best paper airplanes,
with sky-high honors!

You've earned your wings! Now that you've logged dozens
of flying hours in Highlights Flight School and launched
scores of planes, you're ready to fly solo.

Congratulations!

You've graduated
from Highlights
Flight School with
sky-high honors!

Fill out the diploma above
and display it with your
best models.

Cut out your
Ace-Flyer Pilot's License.
Don't forget to add your
photo for identification.

Highlights®
Flight School
Pape*r* Plane*s* That Soa*r*
ACE-FLYER
PILOT'S LICENSE

Your Photo Here

Name_____

Address_____

_____

City_____ State_____ Zip_____

Age ___ Height _____ Weight _____ Eyes _____

To remove, pull firmly along perforated lines.

To remove, pull firmly along perforated lines.

Highlights  Flight School

Highlights Flight School
ACE-FLYER PILOT'S LICENSE

to remove, pull firmly along perforated line.

To remove, pull firmly along perforated line.

To remove, pull firmly along perforated line.

To remove, pull firmly along perforated line.

To remove, pull firmly along perforated line.

To remove, pull firmly along perforated line.

To remove, pull firmly along perforated line.

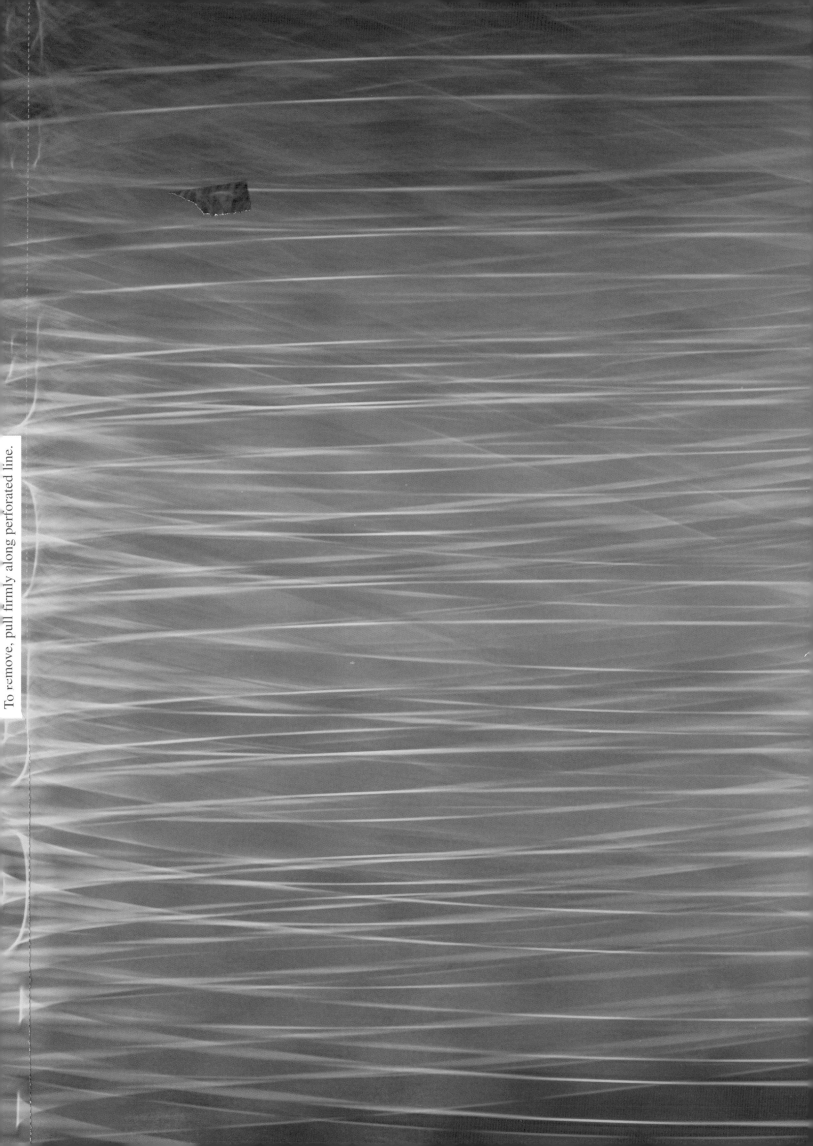

To remove, pull firmly along perforated line.

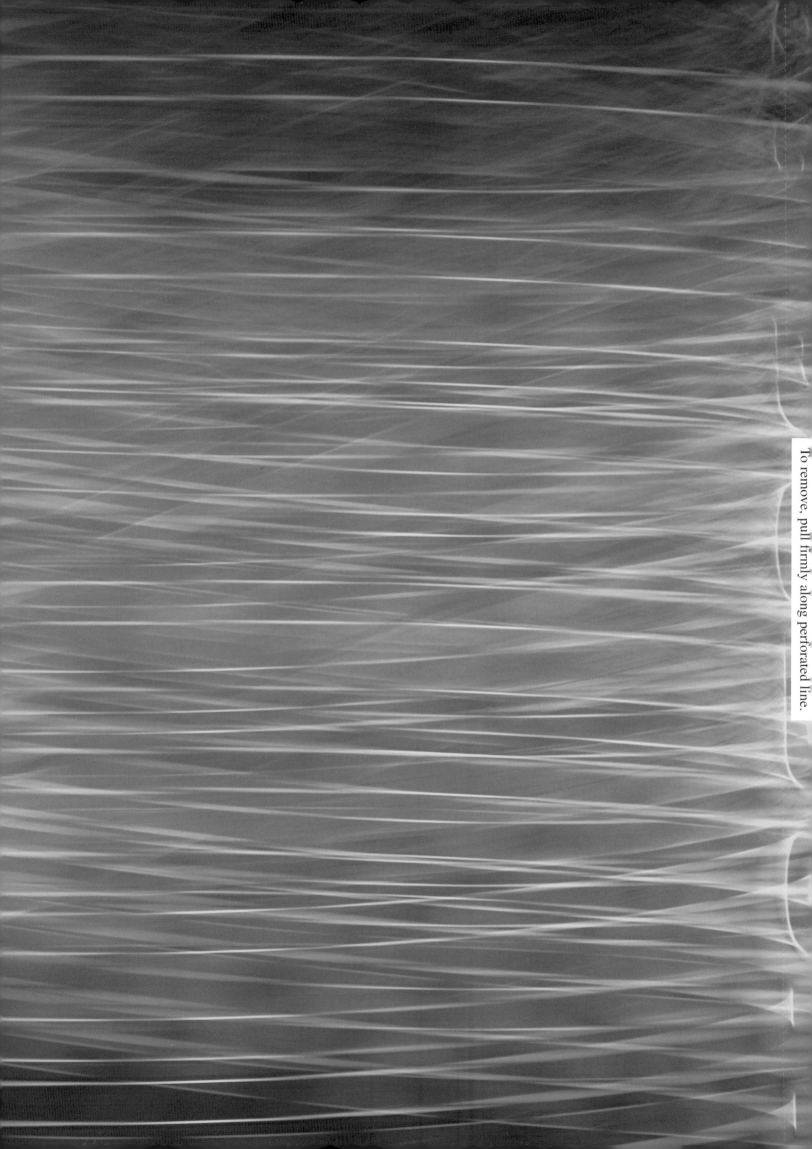

To remove, pull firmly along perforated line.

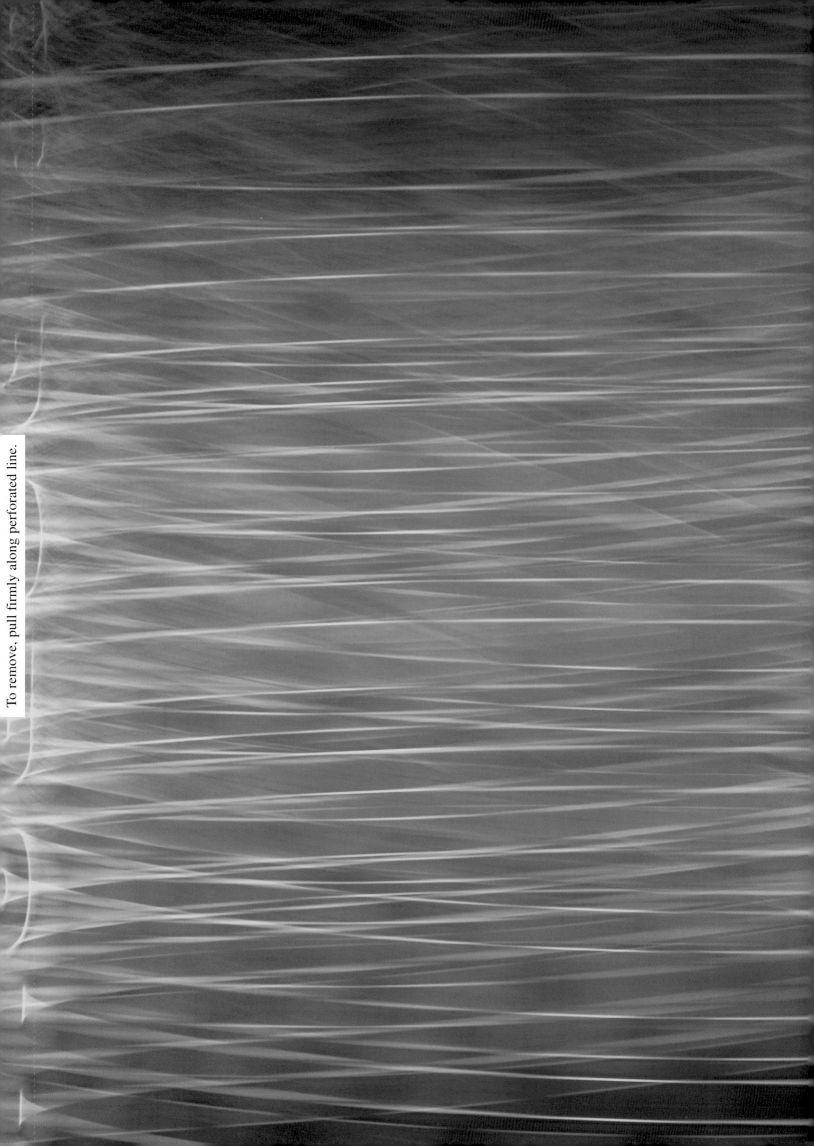

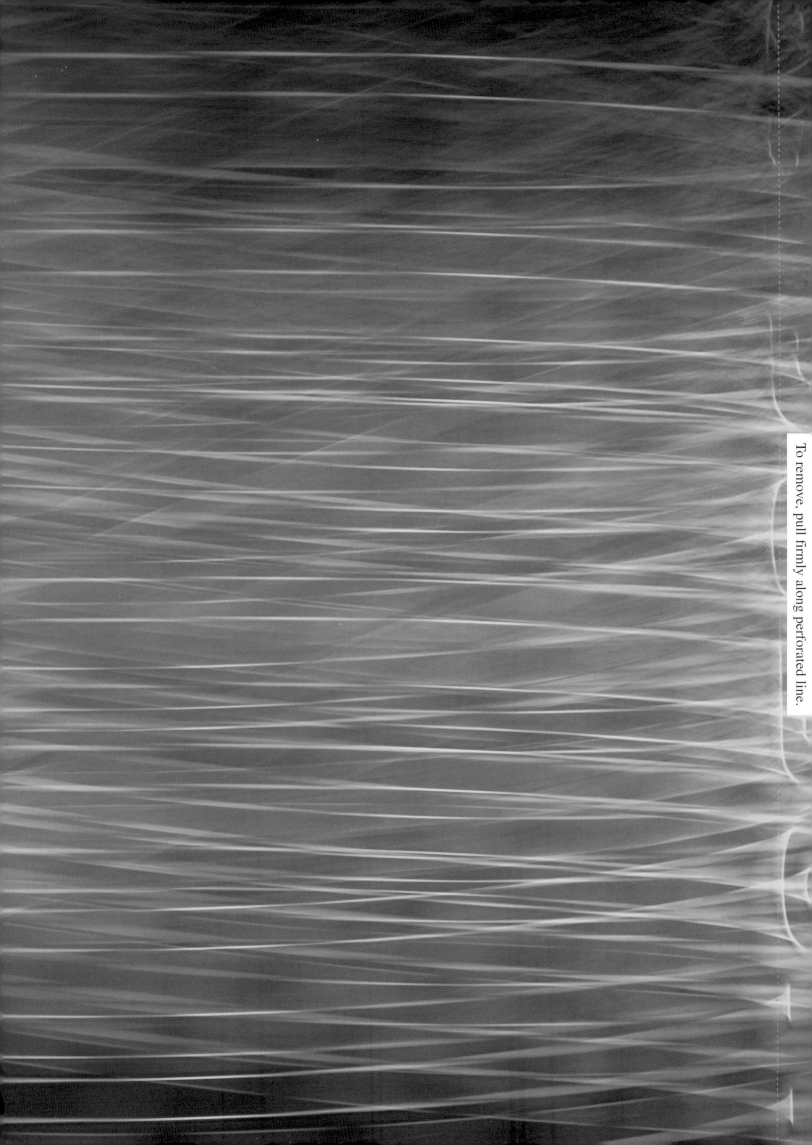

To remove, pull firmly along perforated line.

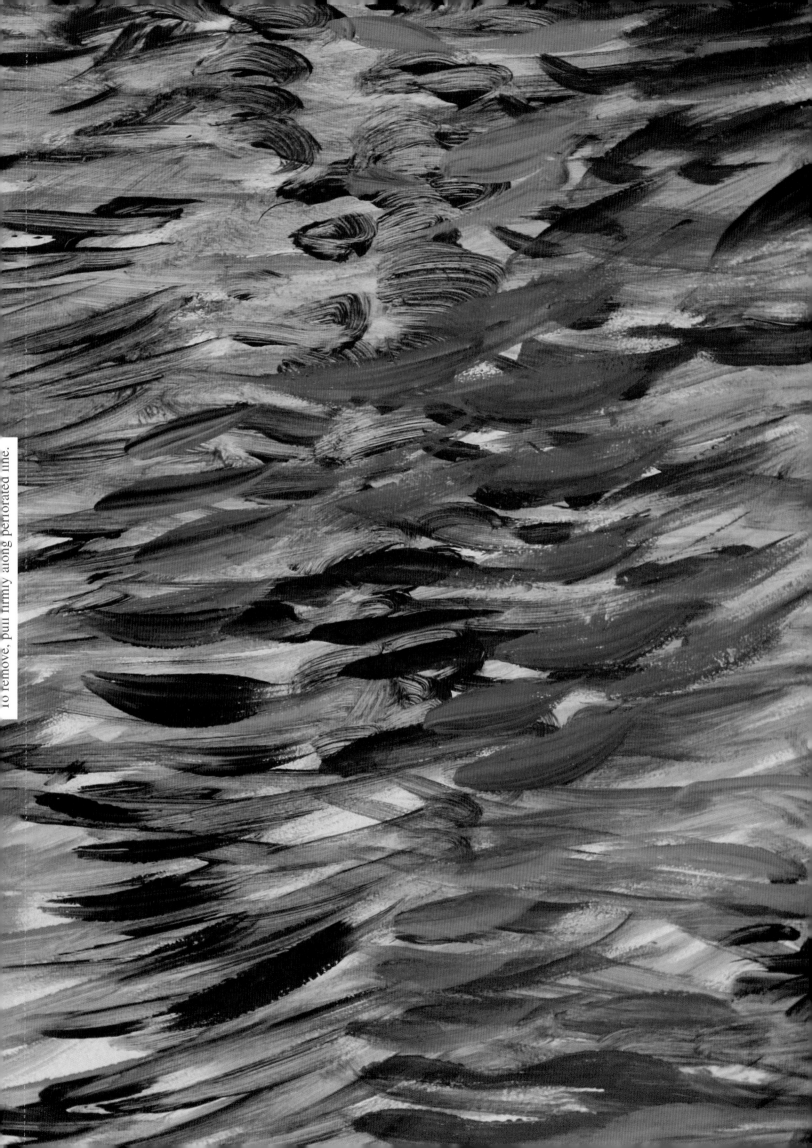

To remove, pull firmly along perforated line.

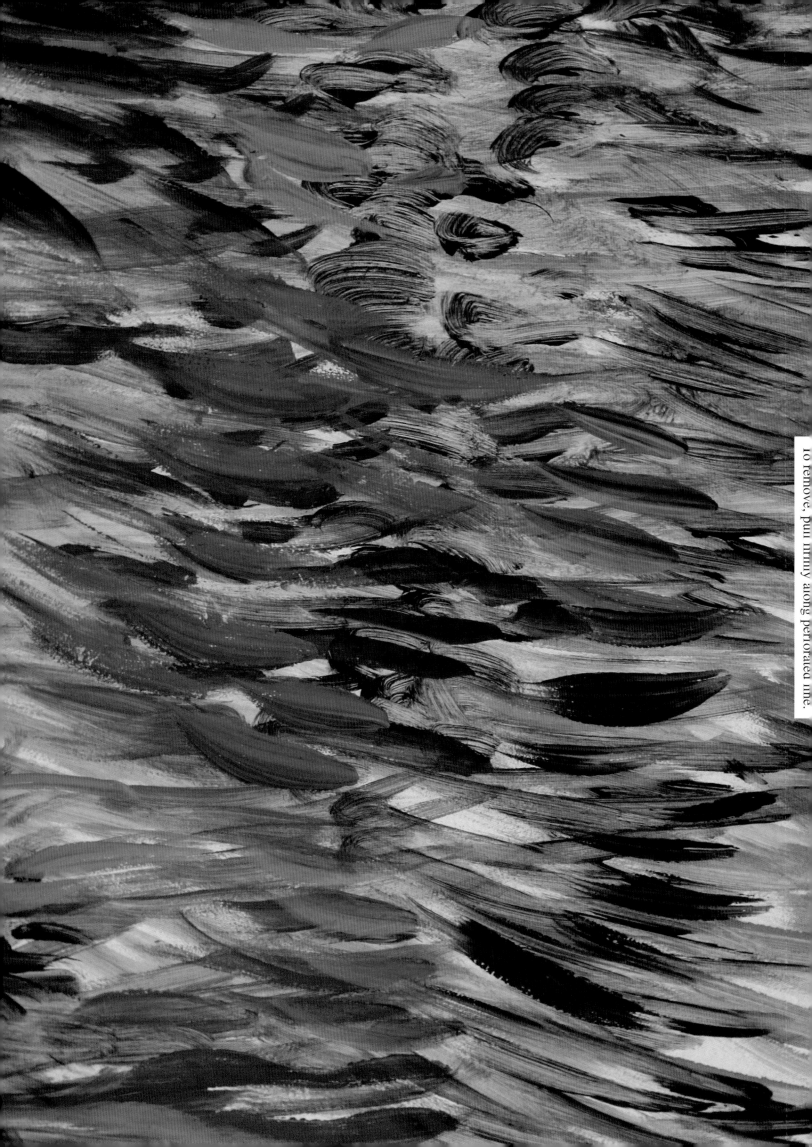

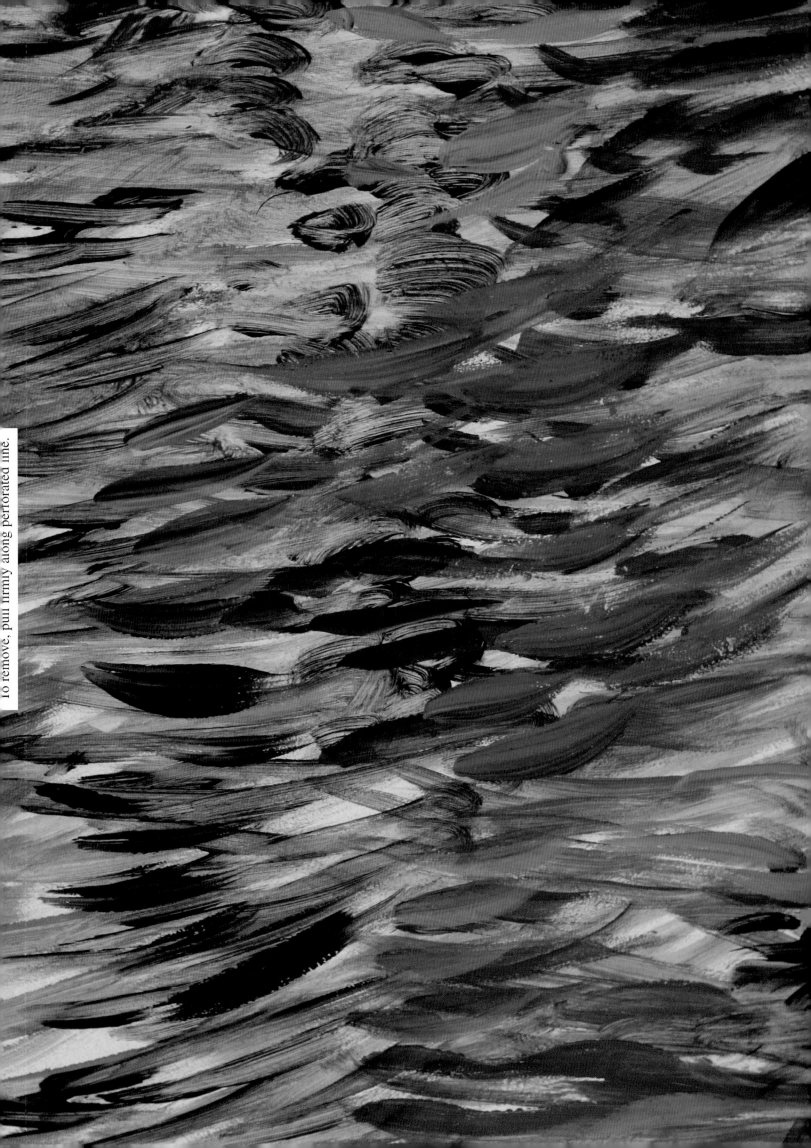

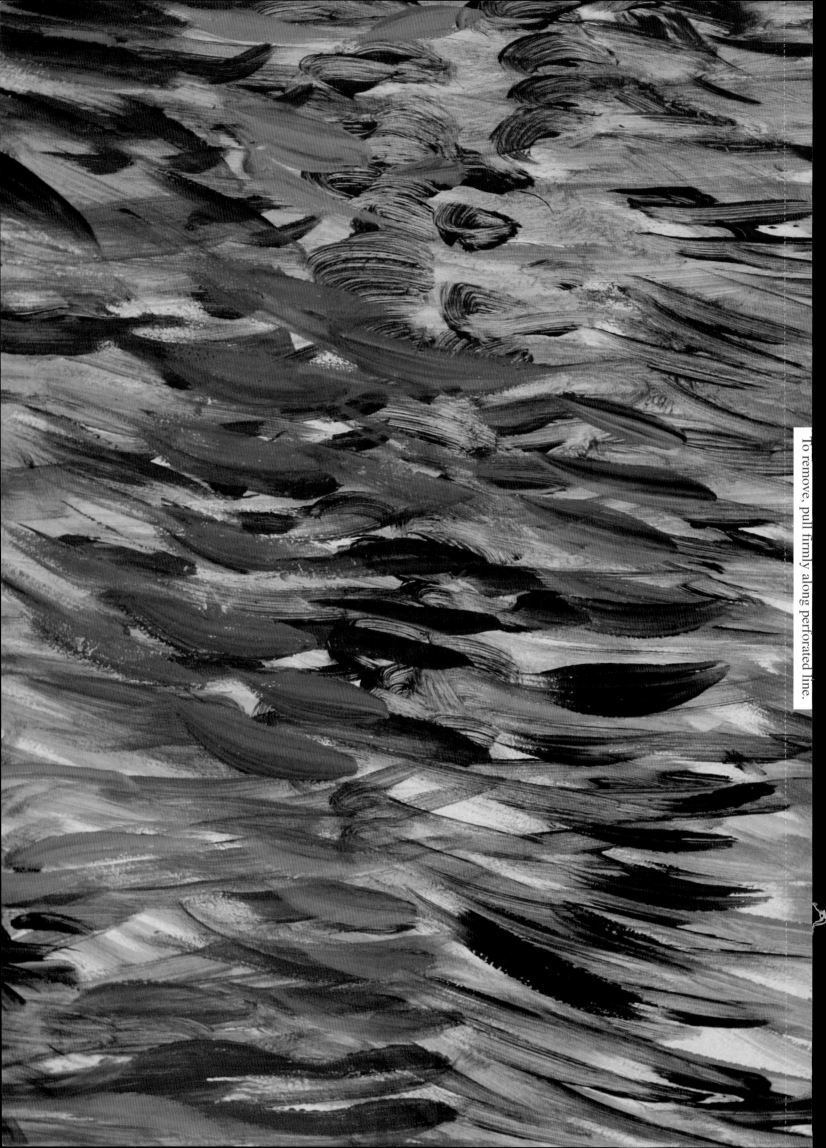

To remove, pull firmly along perforated line.

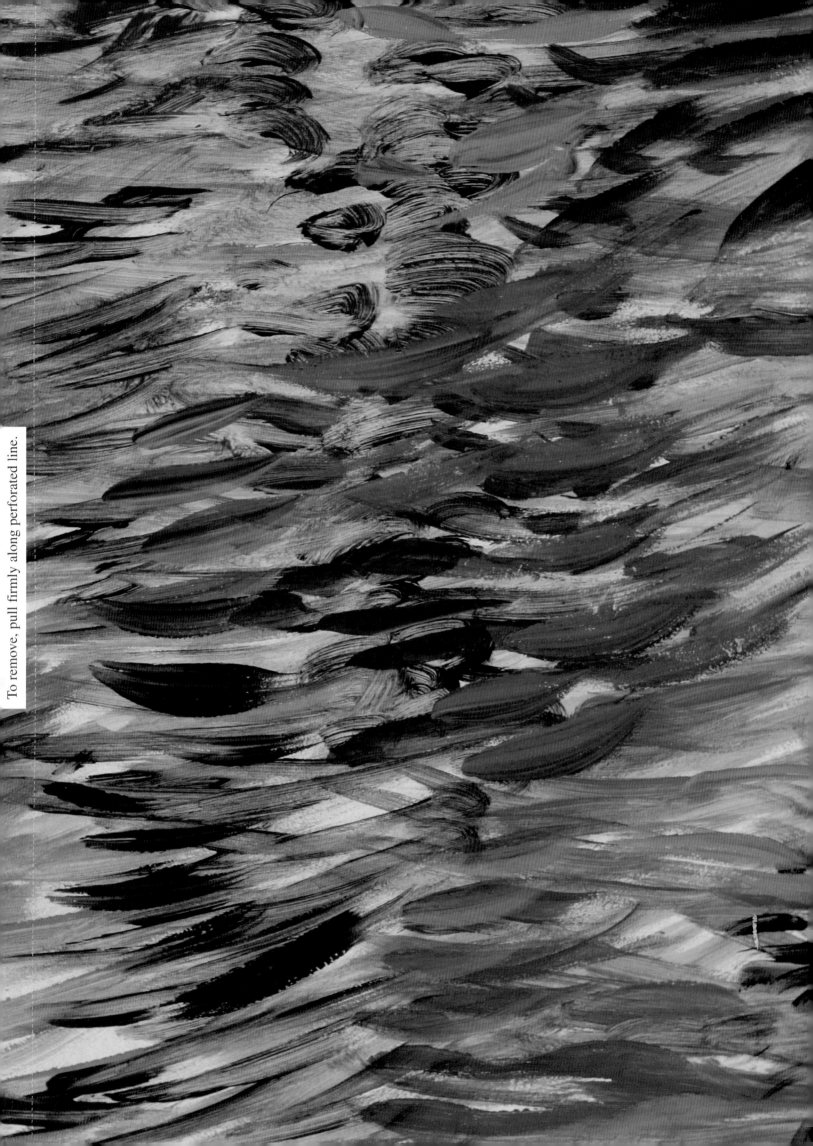

To remove, pull firmly along perforated line.

To remove, pull firmly along perforated line.

To remove, pull firmly along perforated line.

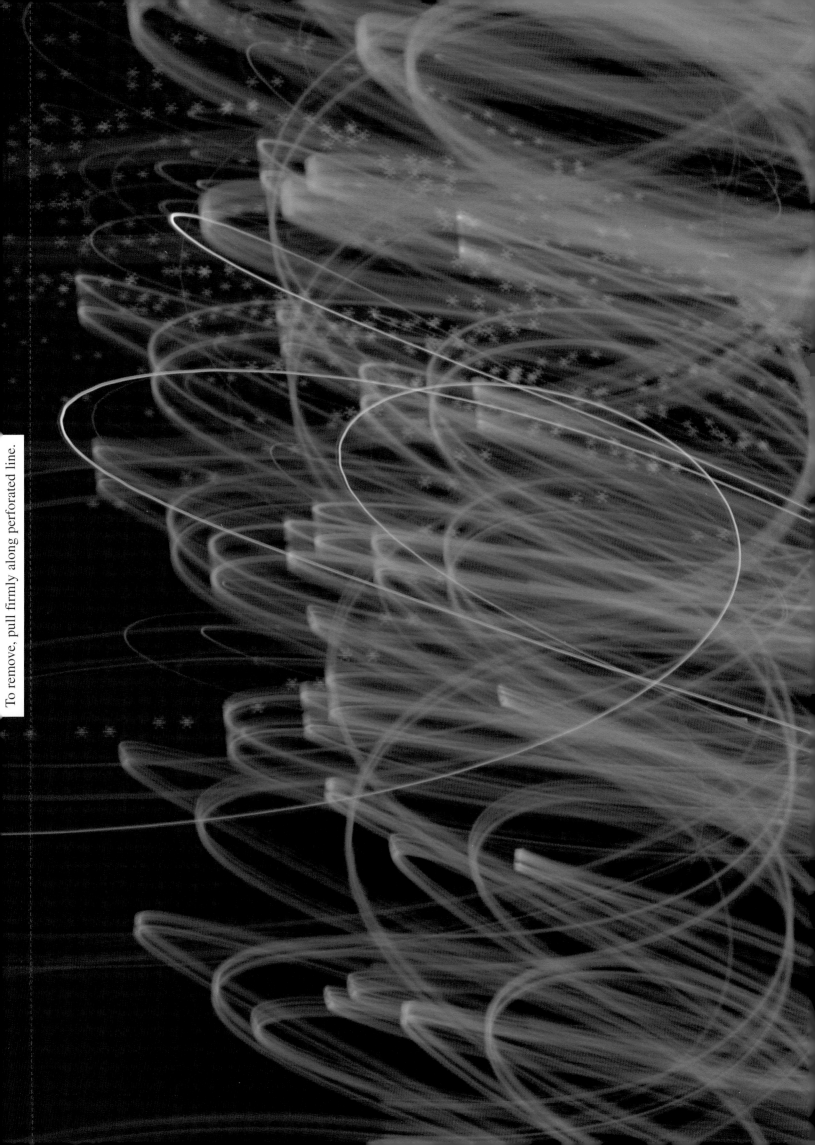

To remove, pull firmly along perforated line.

To remove, pull firmly along perforated line.

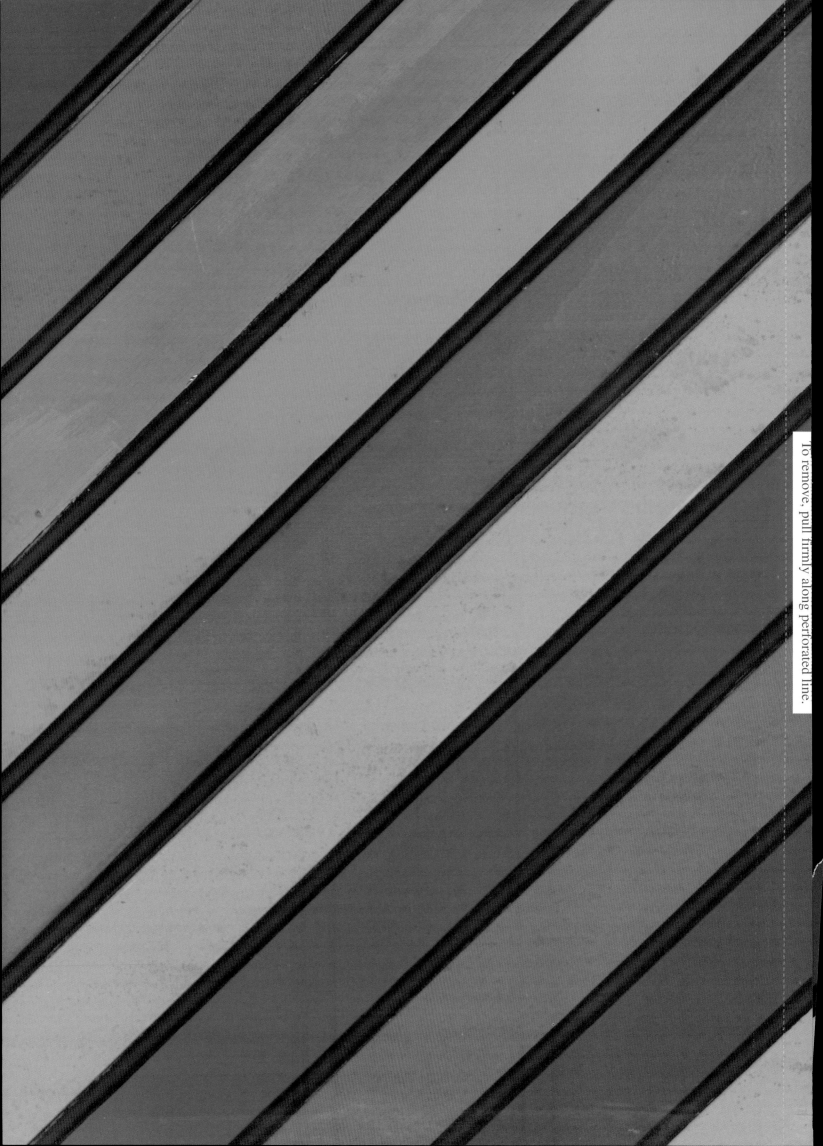

To remove, pull firmly along perforated line.

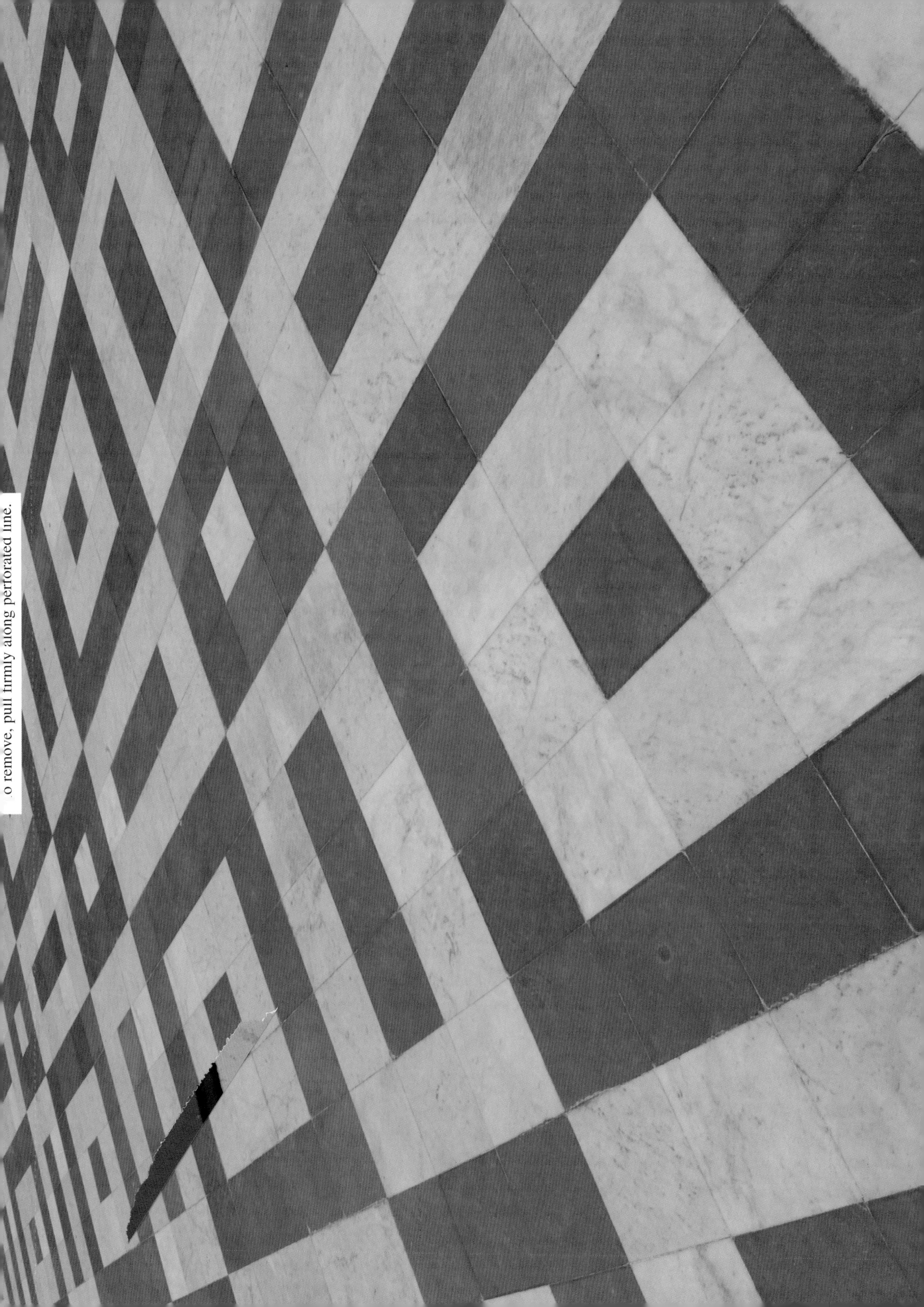

o remove, pull firmly along perforated line.

To remove, pull firmly along perforated line.

To remove, pull firmly along perforated line.

To remove, pull firmly along perforated line.

To remove, pull firmly along perforated line.

To remove, pull firmly along perforated line.

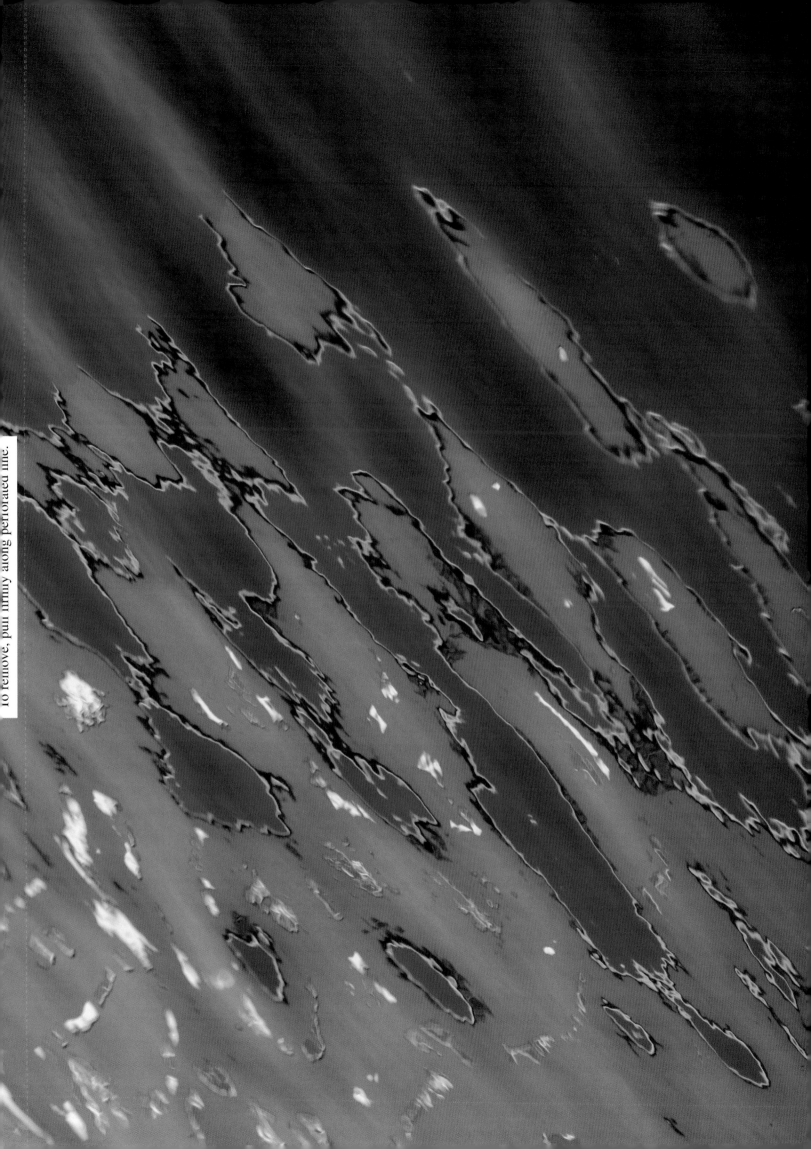

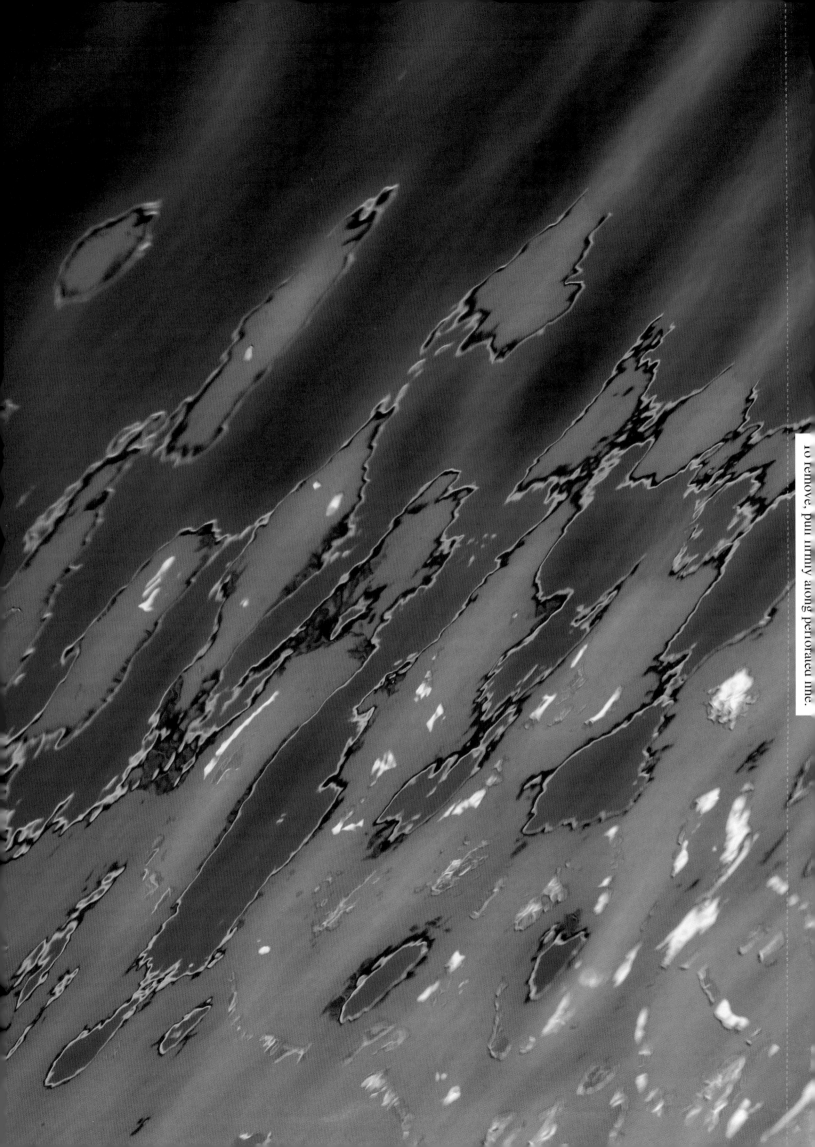

To remove, pull firmly along perforated line.

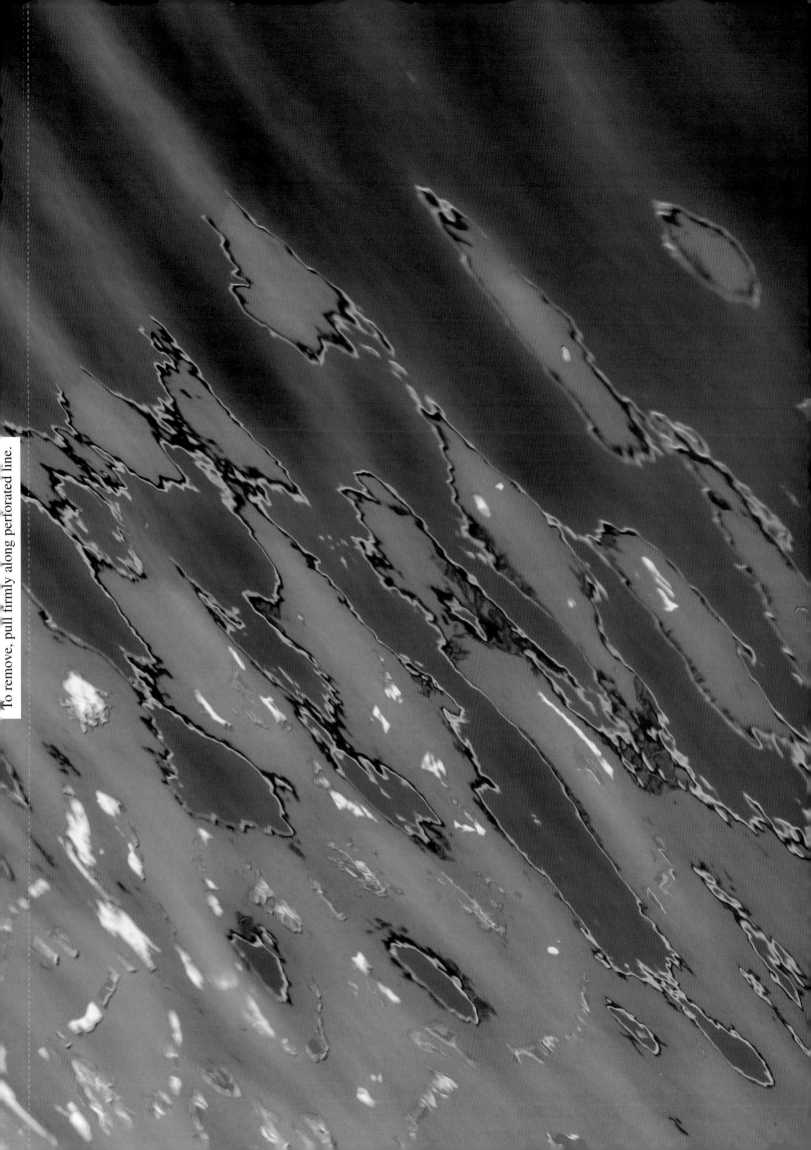

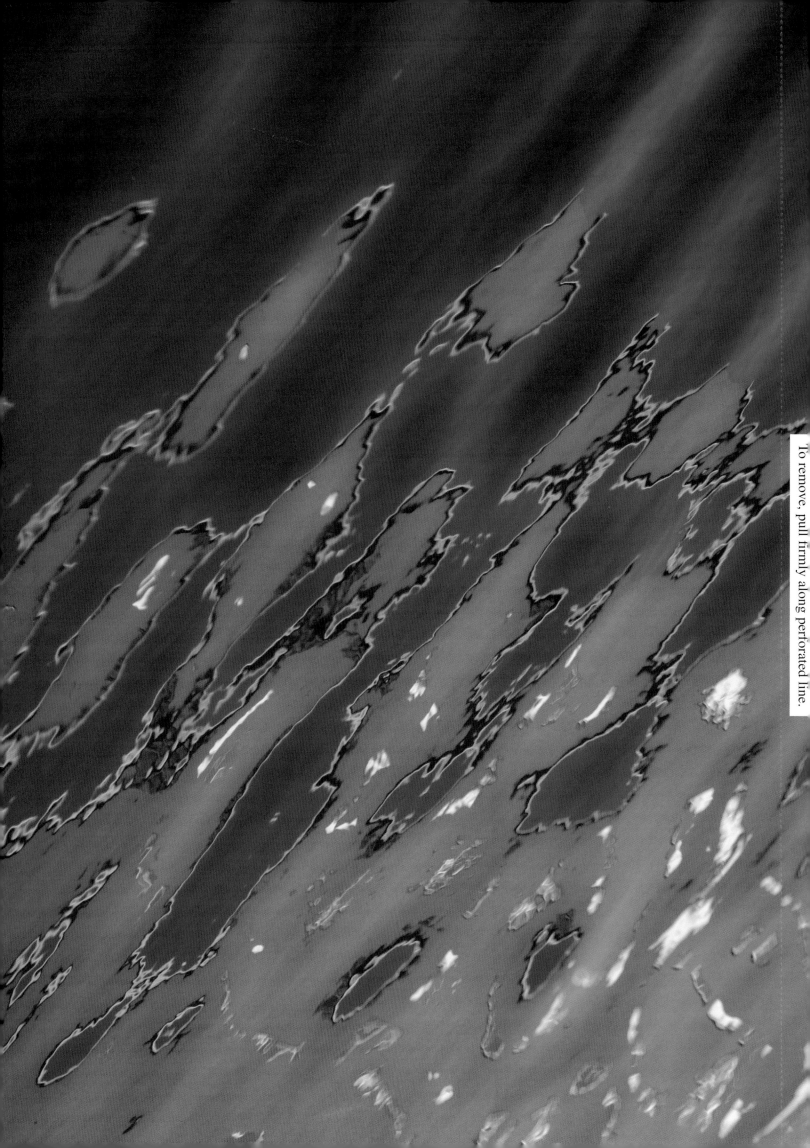

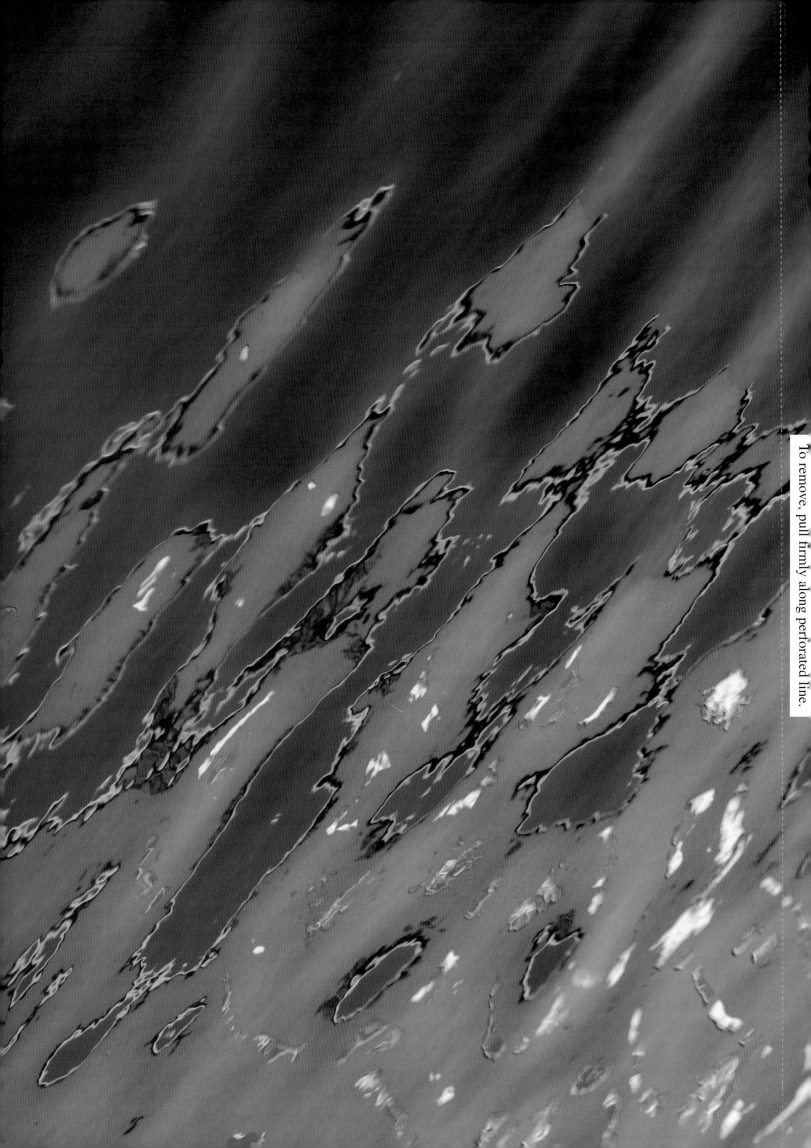

To remove, pull firmly along perforated line.

To remove, pull firmly along perforated line.

To remove, pull firmly along perforated line.

To review, pin money above periodic line.

To remove, pull firmly along perforated line.

To remove, pull firmly along perforated line.

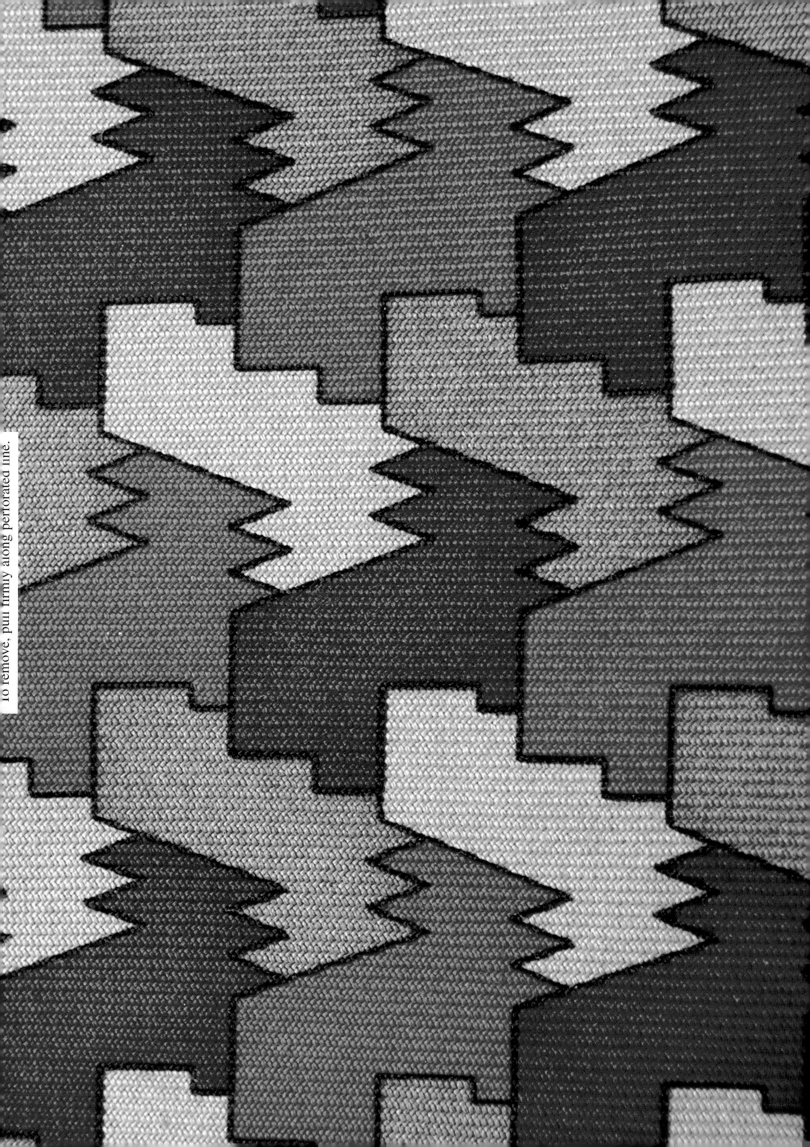

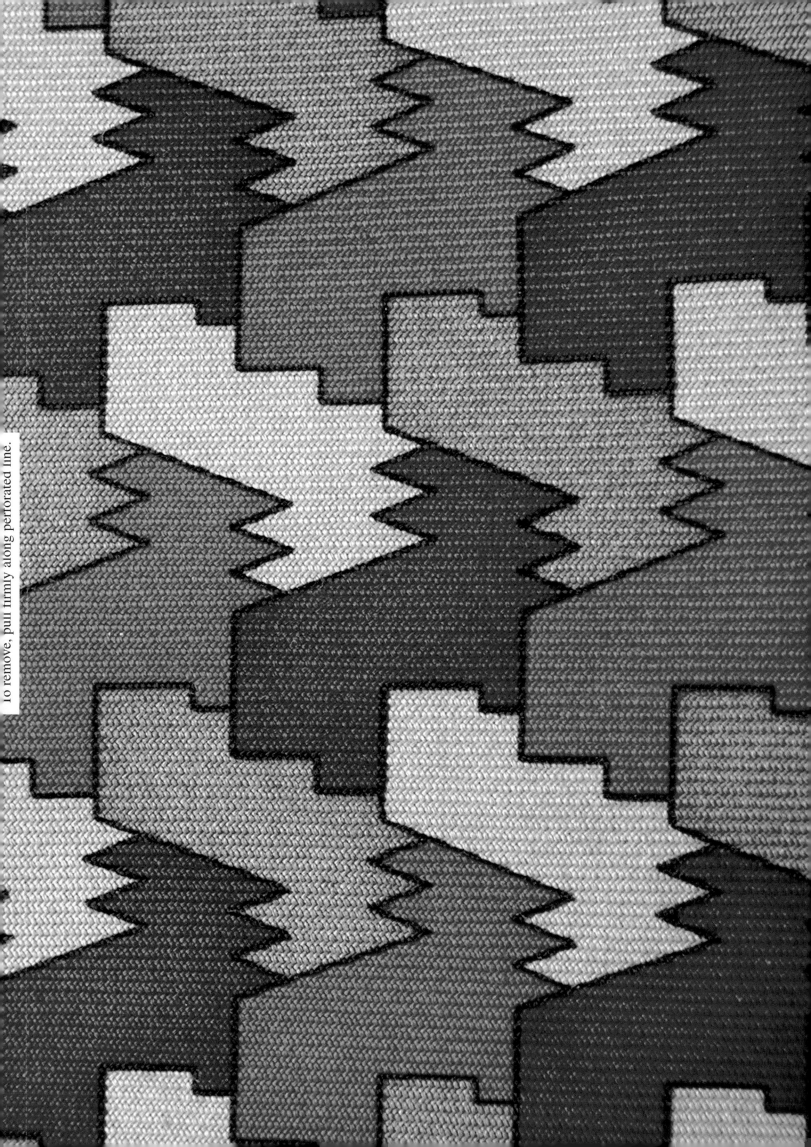

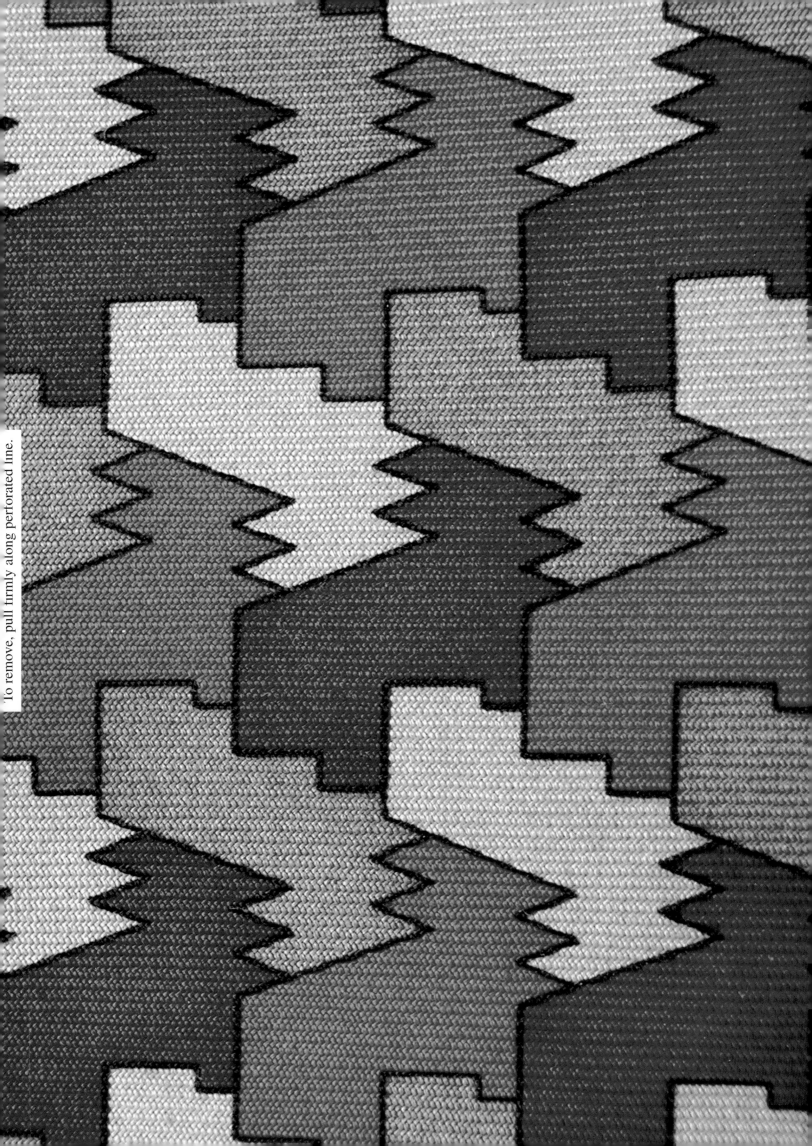

To remove, pull firmly along perforated line.

To remove, pull firmly along perforated line.

to remove, pull firmly along perforated line.

To remove, pull firmly along perforated line.

To remove, pull firmly along perforated line.

To remove, pull firmly along perforated line.

To remove, pull firmly along perforated line.

To remove, pull firmly along perforated line.

To remove, pull firmly along perforated line.

To remove, pull firmly along perforated line.

To remove, pull firmly along perforated line.

To remove, pull firmly along perforated line.

To remove, pull firmly along perforated line.

To remove, pull firmly along perforated line.

To remove, pull firmly along perforated line.

To remove, pull firmly along perforated line.

to remove, pull firmly along perforated line.

To remove, pull firmly along perforated line.

To remove, pull firmly along perforated line.

To remove, pull firmly along perforated line.

to remove, and many along perforated line.

To remove, pull firmly along perforated line.

To remove, pull firmly along perforated line.

To remove, pull firmly along perforated line.

to remove, pull firmly along perforated line.

To remove, pull firmly along perforated line.

To remove, pull firmly along perforated line.

To remove, pull firmly along perforated line.

To remove, pull firmly along perforated line.

To remove, pull firmly along perforated line.

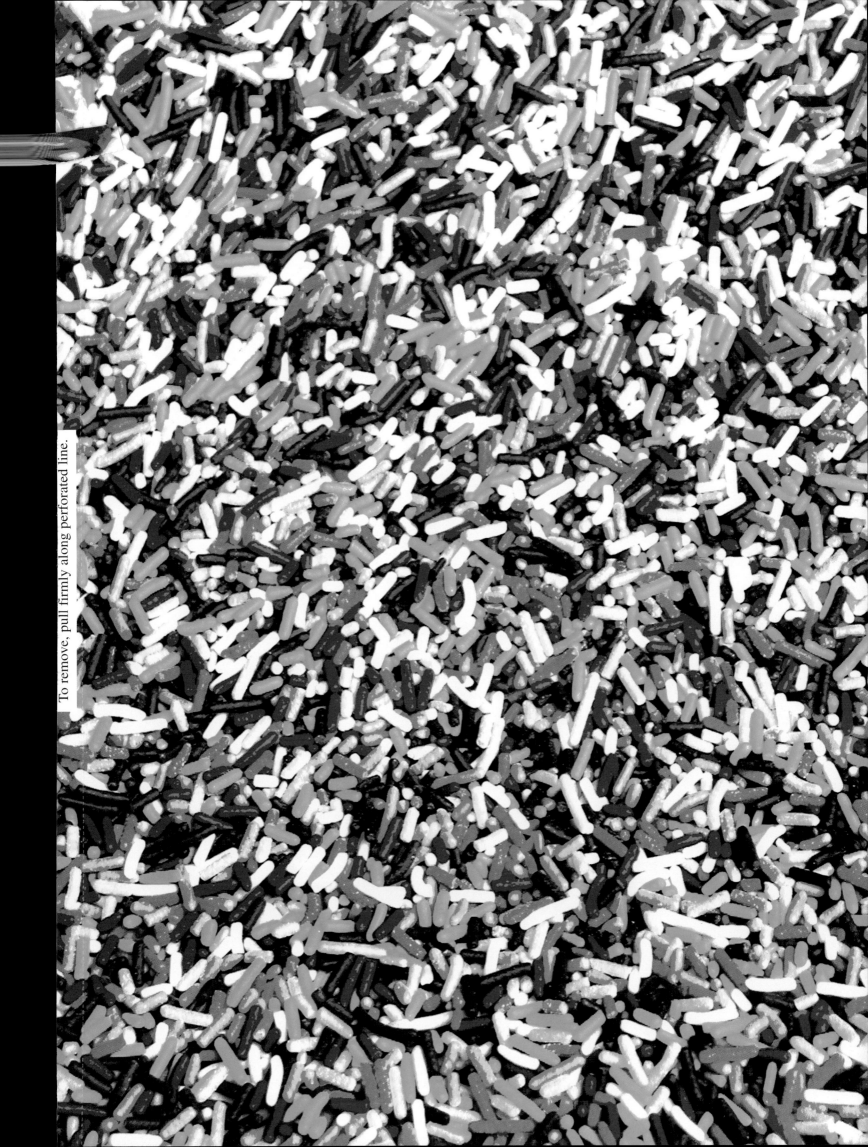

To remove, pull firmly along perforated line.

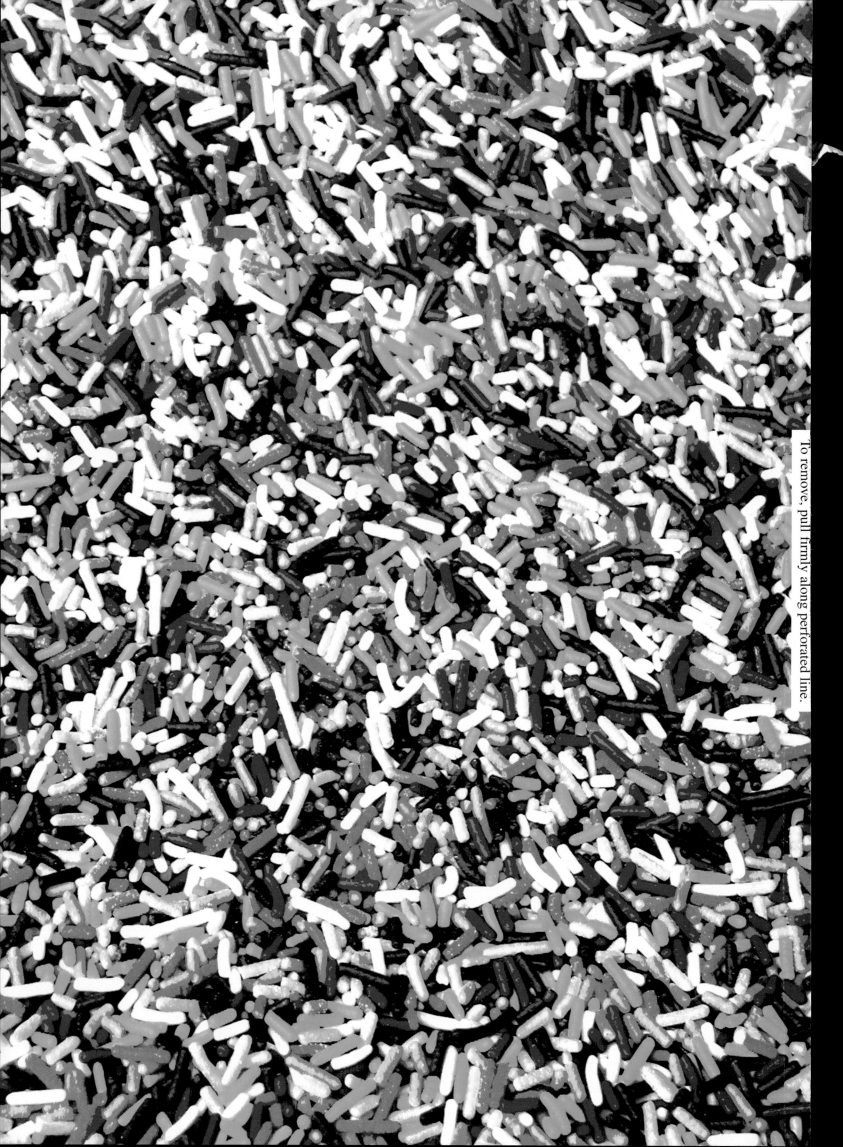

To remove, pull firmly along perforated line.

To remove, pull firmly along perforated line.

To remove, pull firmly along perforated line.

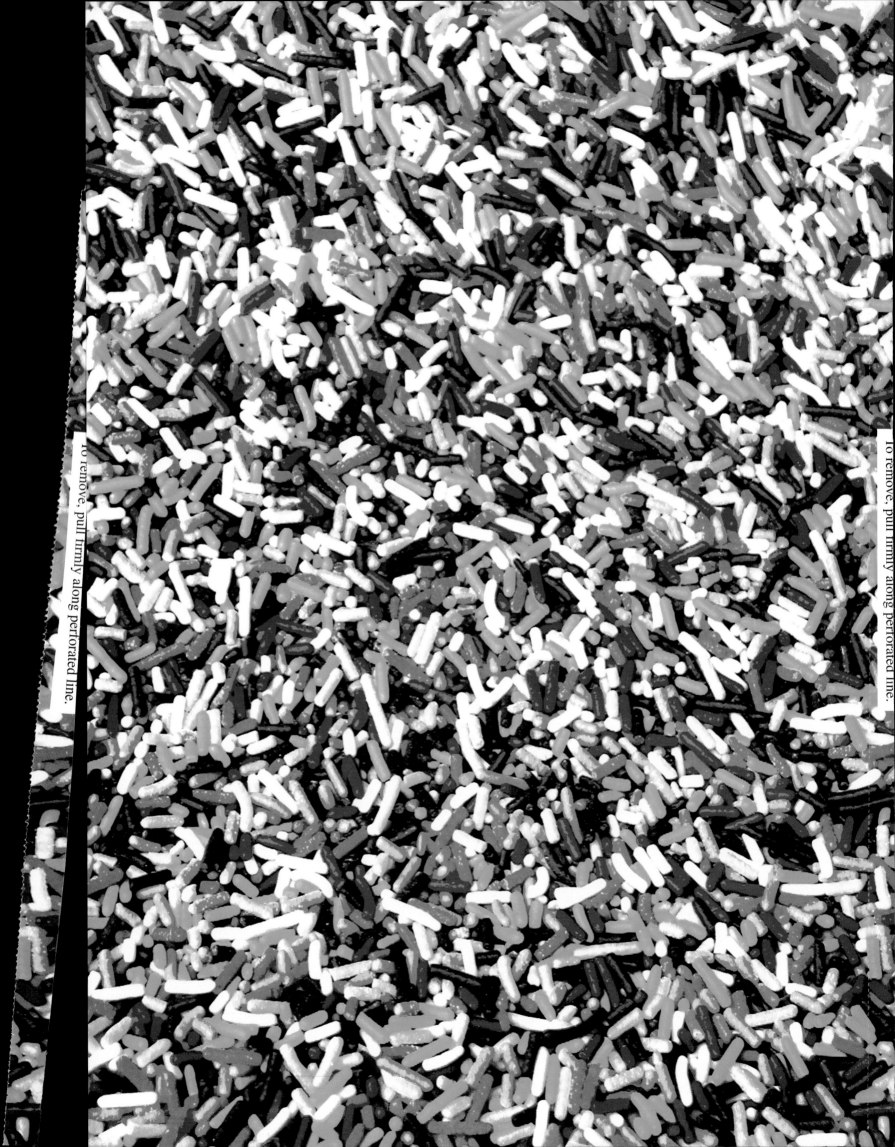

To remove, pull firmly along perforated line.

To remove, pull firmly along perforated line.

To remove, pull firmly along perforated line.

To remove, pull firmly along perforated line.

To remove, pull firmly along perforated line.

To remove, pull firmly along perforated line.

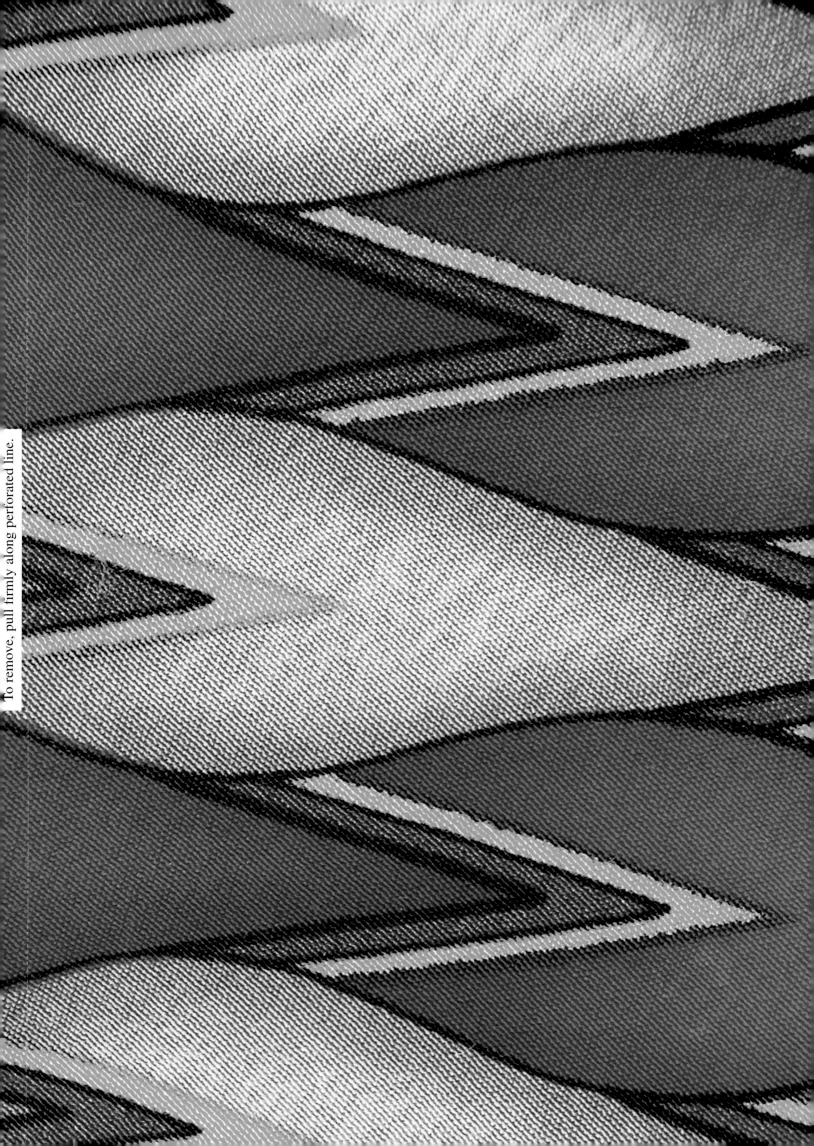

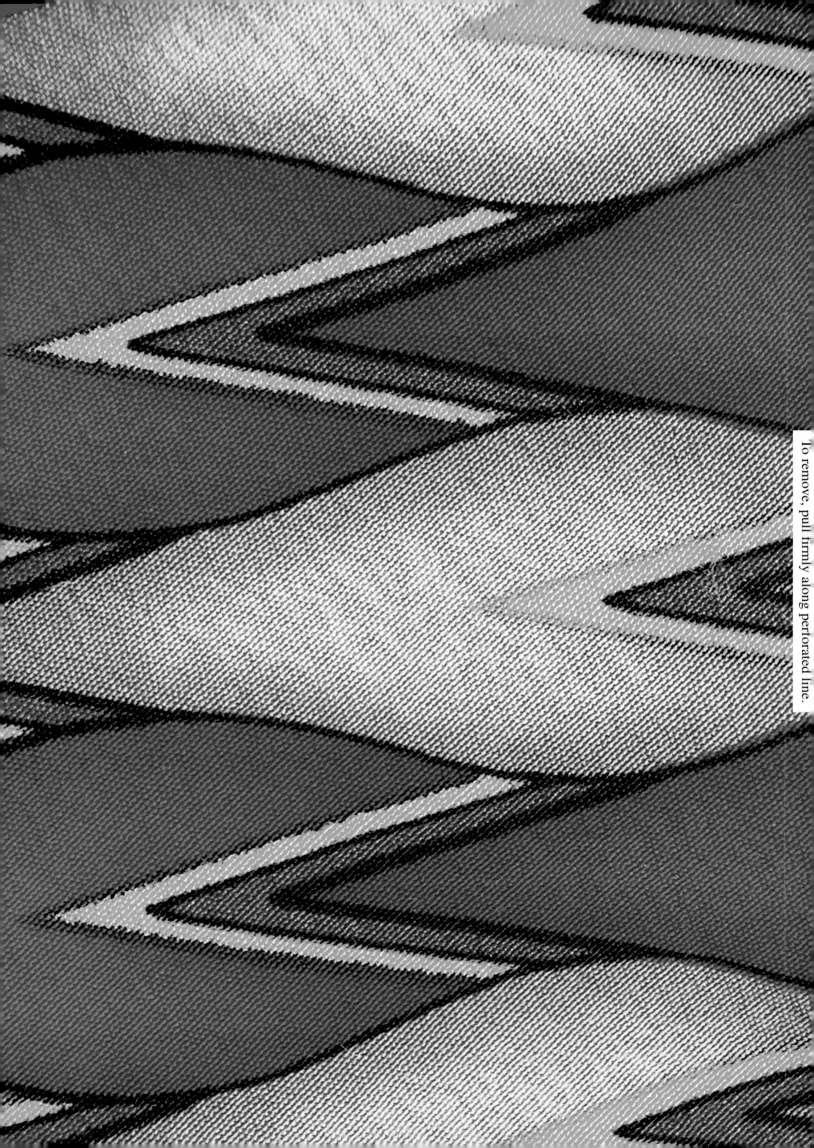

To remove, pull firmly along perforated line.

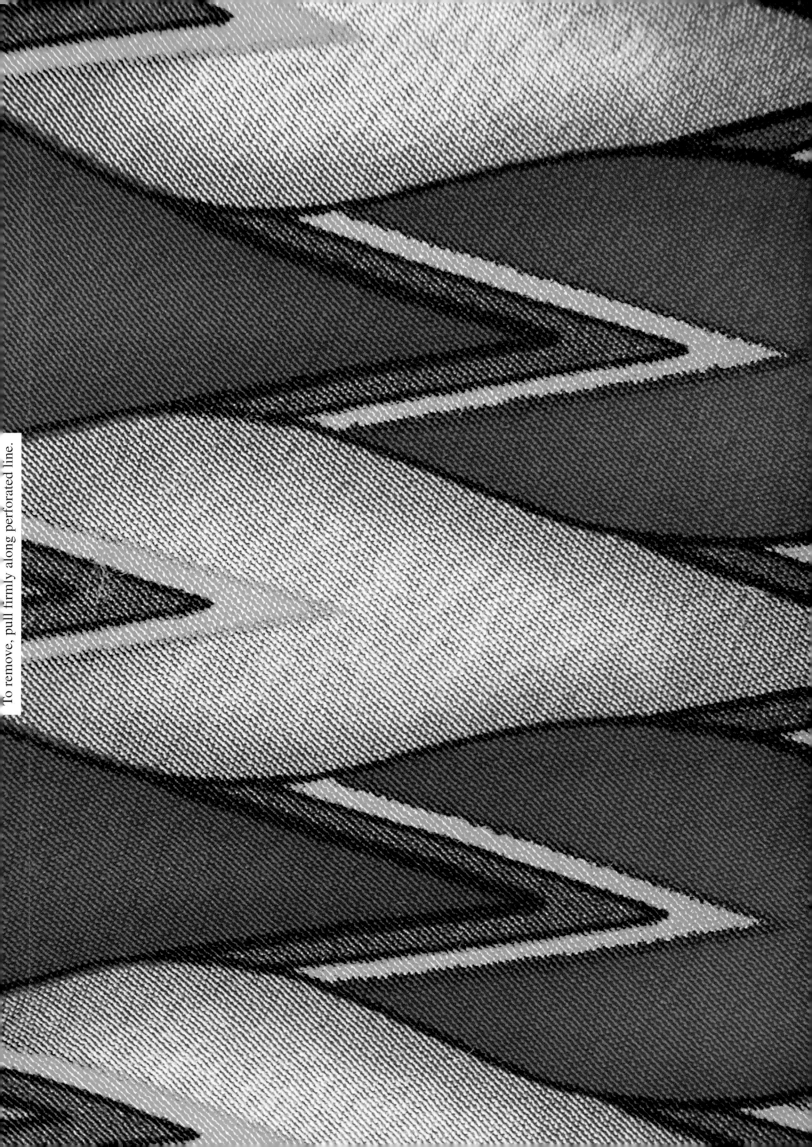

To remove, pull firmly along perforated line.

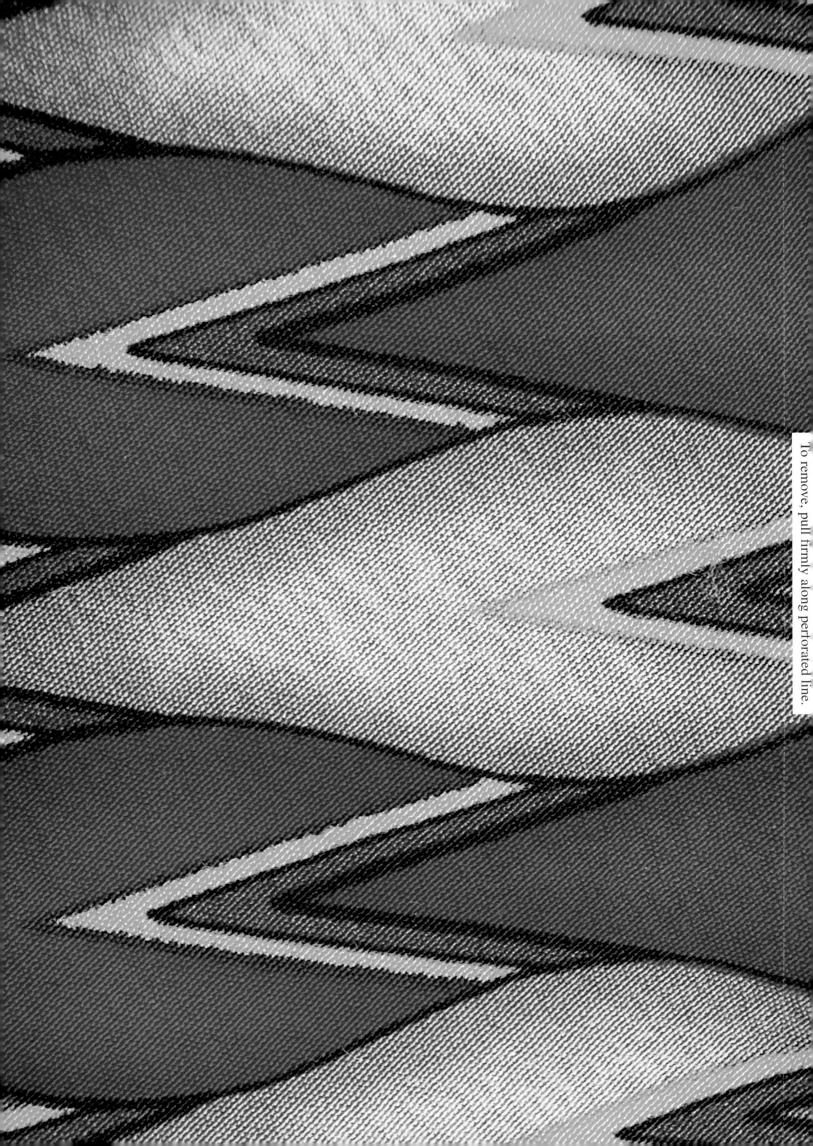

To remove, pull firmly along perforated line.

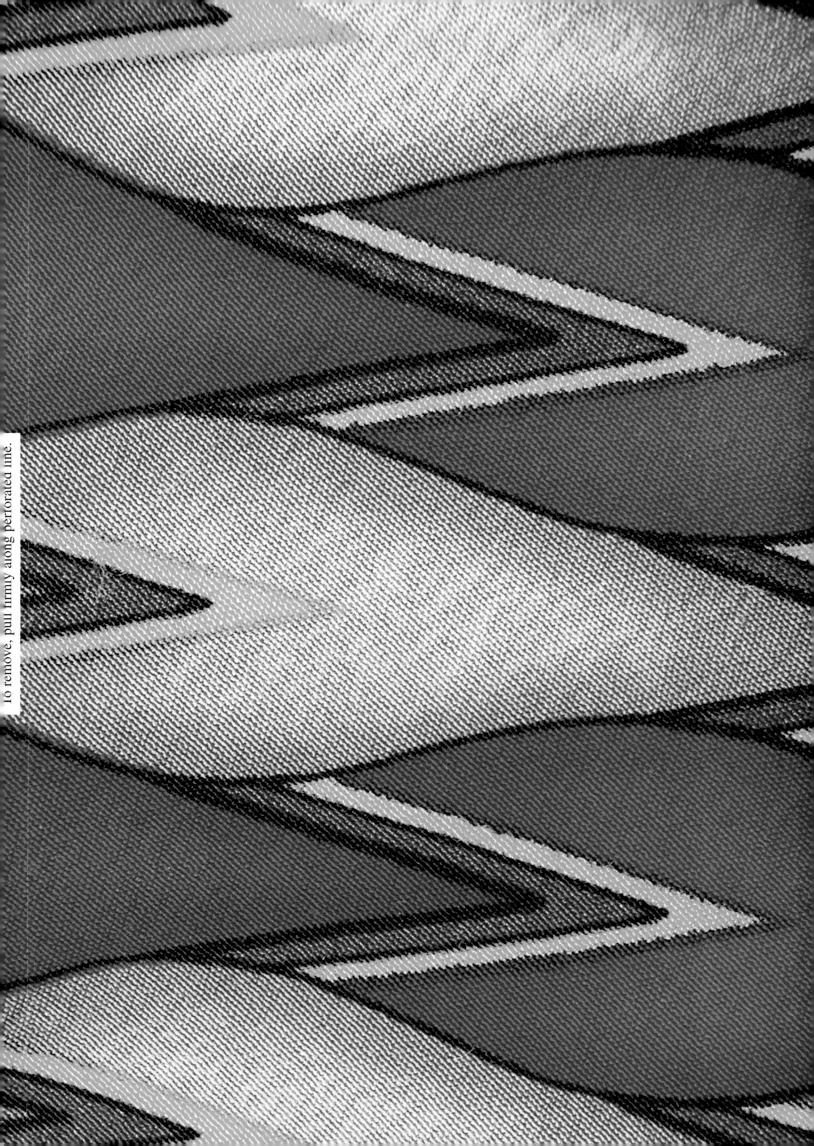

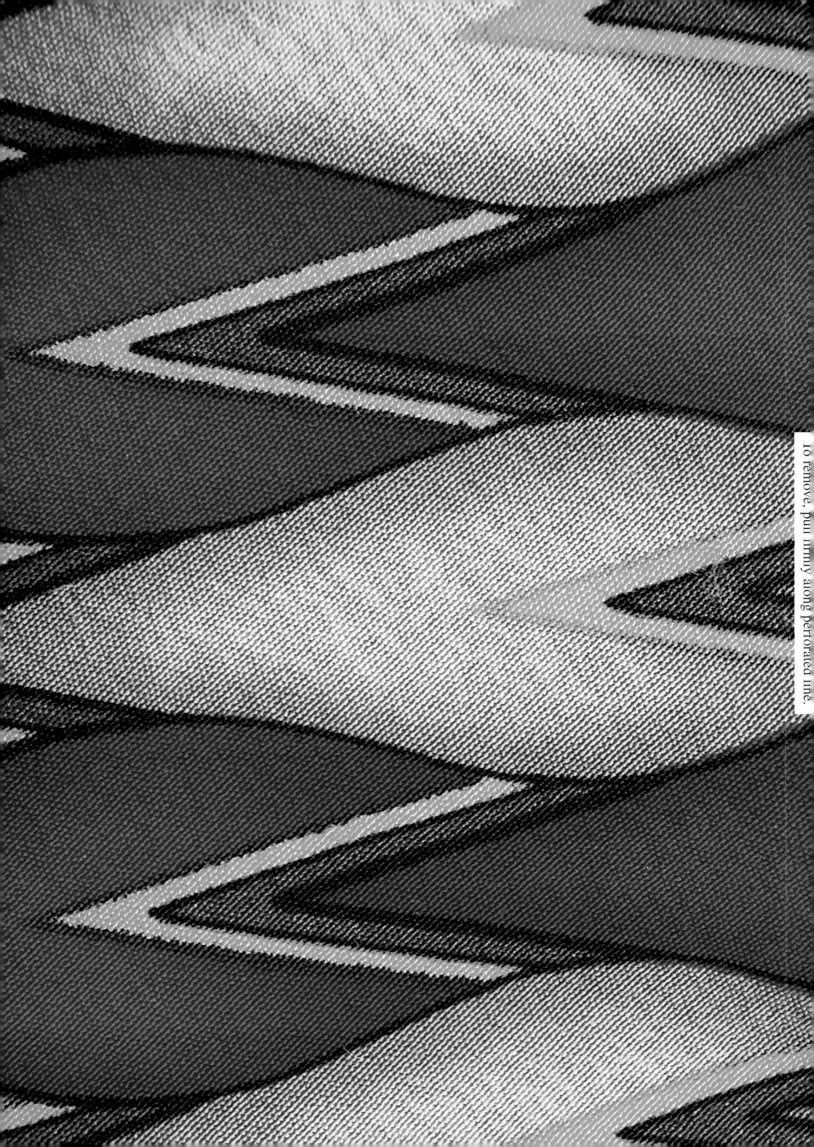

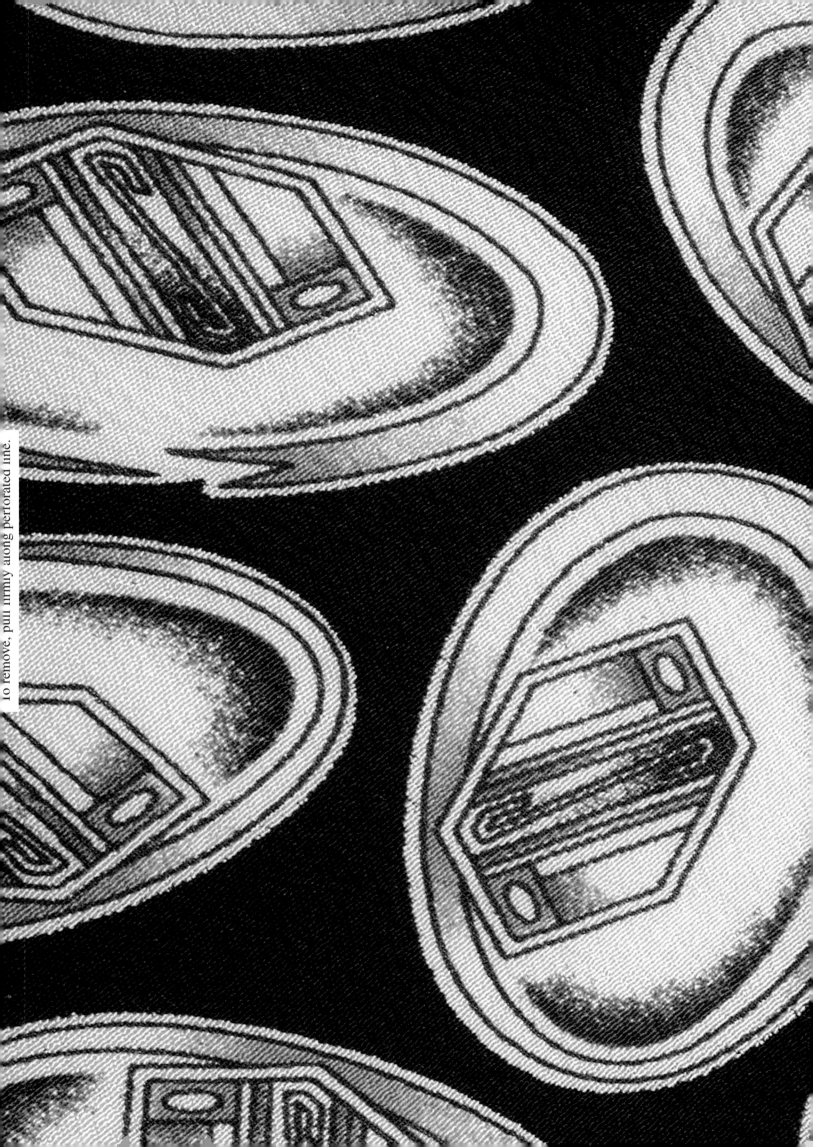

To remove, pull firmly along perforated line.

To remove, pull firmly along perforated line.

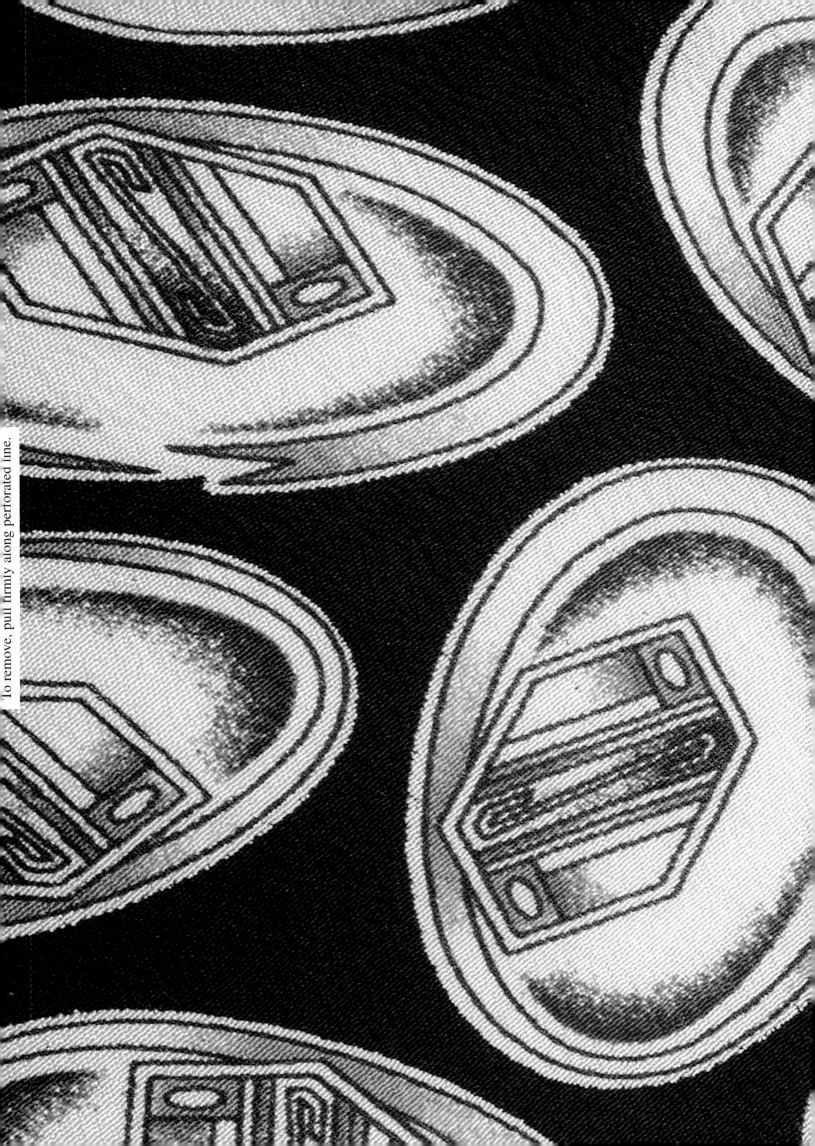

To remove, pull firmly along perforated line.